The Wines of
Long Island

The Wines of Long Island

by
Edward Beltrami and
Philip F. Palmedo

Photographs by
Sara Matthews

Preface by
Paul Pontallier
General Manager, Château Margaux

Amereon House
MATTITUCK, NEW YORK

International Standard Book Number 0-8488-2765-1

To order contact:
AMEREON HOUSE,
the publishing division of
Amereon Ltd.
Post Office Box 1200
Mattituck, New York 11952-9500

Manufactured by The Peconic Companies
Mattituck, New York

 Contents

# Acknowledgements

*T*his new edition of *The Wines of Long Island* continues to embody the contributions of many friends and advisors acknowledged in the first edition. The editorial advice of Charles Nichols in the first edition and Chris Palmedo in both versions helped to clarify the text. The support and encouragement of our wives, Barbara Beltrami and Betsy Palmedo, transcend editions.

Generous written comments by Antonia Booth, Historian of the Town of Southold, allowed us to correct and extend our historical account. In recent years the combined work of three journalists have provided an invaluable living history of Long Island's wine industry. We are not alone in missing the irrepressibly irreverent *GrapeZine* and its late editor, Michael Todd. Happily, Howard Goldberg, in the somewhat more august *New York Times*, continues to write insightful and robust articles about the people and events shaping the future of the region. We have also been informed by Alan J. Wax's knowledgeable columns in *Newsday*.

Once more, we drink a toast of thanks to Long Island's winery owners, vineyard managers and winemakers who were unfailingly generous with their time and their knowledge. They have created an important new wine region and have given fresh life to a beautiful corner of the earth.

 Preface

I was first introduced to winemaking on Long Island when I had the pleasure of participating in the Symposium on Maritime Climate Winegrowing that was held on the beautiful East End in July, 1988. I was struck by several things during the days I spent on Long Island that summer: the strong connections with our winemaking traditions in Bordeaux, the kindness and the adventurous spirit of the winemakers and vineyard owners and the remarkable quality of the wines.

We are very proud of the centuries-old traditions that we carry forward as we make wines in France. The qualities of our wines derive from those traditions and the superb endowments of soil and weather with which we are blessed. But those inheritances - and the laws that control our winemaking practices - are also constraints on our freedom. I must confess that I was somewhat envious of the freedom with which Long Island wine makers could approach the creation of an entirely new wine region. At the same time, I was impressed by the knowledge and respect that Long Island's winemakers had concerning winemaking practices and traditions in other parts of the world, particularly Bordeaux.

I detected on Long Island a strong sense of community - both from a local perspective, and with the broader wine-making community of the world. My visit there was brief, but I felt I made friends among these knowledgeable, enthusiastic, hospitable, warm Long Island winemakers.

And I was impressed, very impressed by the quality of the wines that I tasted on Long Island, particularly some beautiful Merlots and Chardonnays. On the French time scale, Long Island is in its infancy as a wine region, and it will be years, if not decades, before its full potential is realized. But its promise is formidable.

I am delighted that those qualities of the new Long Island wine region that struck me at the time of my first visit: the kindness and adventurous spirit of the people, the reflections of winemaking traditions in France, the beauty of the region and the high quality of the wines have now been so well captured by Philip Palmedo's and Edward Beltrami's text and through Sara Matthews's sensitive photographs. I only wish that the early, formative days in the history of Bordeaux had been captured with the care, intelligence and affection that come through so clearly in this fine volume.

Paul Pontallier
General Manager, Château Margaux, March 5, 1993

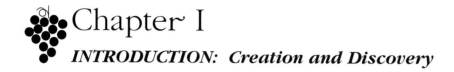

Chapter I

INTRODUCTION: *Creation and Discovery*

"Long Island...there, Colonel Gibbs, from whose garden the Isabella came, amused himself with a vineyard, as did Colonel Spooner; there, poor Loubat struggled and failed to compel vinifera to grow on a commercial scale; and there the learned Prince poured out, through his catalogues and monographs, information to the country at large..."

—Thomas Pinney
A History of Wine in America from the Beginnings to Prohibition

This book was written to serve two purposes. First, it is a history of America's youngest major wine region. At the same time it is a visitor's guide to the wineries that now are scattered through Long Island's bucolic East End. We also describe the grapes, the vineyard practices and winemaking techniques used on Long Island that connect the region to the great European winemaking traditions.

Creation is an apt term to describe the activities of the wine pioneers, investors, grape growers and winemakers who have turned the East End of Long Island into the most exciting new wine region in the country. Discovery is also an apt descriptor. Michelangelo described his sculptural process as the release of forms latent in the marble. Many of Long Island's winemakers feel the same way. They are convinced that the region has very special endowments of climate and soil, and that noble wines are latent here, waiting to be discovered.

Alex and Louisa Hargrave were the first of the modern viticultural pioneers to suspect the latent potential in the soils of eastern Long Island. The original spark struck on Thanksgiving, 1972, when they stopped by the Wickham Fruit Farm on the North Fork. They had been searching both coasts for a favorable place to grow grapes and make wine. When they saw the fresh vegetables brought in from the nearby fields on that mild November day, they knew they had found, in Louisa's words, "a little garden of Eden."

Like many great discoveries, the logic of the Hargrave's decision seems obvious in retrospect. They recognized that the waters of Long Island Sound and the Atlantic produce a climate on the East End of Long Island that is remarkably similar to the climate of Bordeaux, some 5,000 miles to the East. The soils, well-drained, sandy loam, seemed ideal. They planted the grape varieties that produced many of the great wines of the world: cabernet sauvignon, merlot, pinot noir, chardonnay and riesling.

THE WINES OF LONG ISLAND

In the late 1970s, word of interesting wines started to percolate back from the East End. Soon other pioneer winemakers followed in the Hargraves' footsteps. By the mid-1980s, Long Island wines started to catch the attention of wine experts. Even in its early years, Leon D. Adams recognized the potential of the region, and in his authoritative *Wines of America*, published in 1985, he proclaimed that "the still largely rural eastern half of Long Island [could be] the future Pauillac and Côte d'Or of New York." Increasingly, Long Island wines appeared on the wine lists of New York's upscale restaurants. The New York wine public, among the most sophisticated in the world, was beginning to realize that a major wine region was at their doorstep. Never before had a wine region and its reputation grown as fast.

The men and women who are the principal players in this story are an extraordinarily diverse group of people: a computer engineer, who learned how to make wine in Kuwait; a local contractor; a fifth generation Long Island farmer; an Italian prince; the granddaughter of a one time Socialist Presidential candidate; and young winemakers who learned their craft in France, Germany, California, and Australia. They are now competing with each other to make and sell the finest wines, but their common concerns and visions, and the common traditions on which they draw, are creating a rich culture similar to those of the world's traditional wine growing regions.

Tardif's vegetable stand

If Long Island reminds you of a region in France it will probably be Burgundy. While Bordeaux, with its grand châteaux imperiously set among ageless vineyards, may epitomize the aristocratic culture of wine, the wines of the more humble and agriculturally oriented Burgundy need pay homage to no one. The modest clothes worn by Burgundy's important towns belie their renown. Gevrey Chambertin, for example, is reached by following a narrow vineyard road just to the West of National Route 74, a few miles south of Dijon. A battered sign whispers, as

2

though from a previous century, that you are approaching Gevrey Chambertin, population 1,850. If it weren't for that hallowed name, one would take this for just another of the innumerable archaic farming villages that dot every region of France. Rising to the West, however, are the slopes that produce one of the most sublime wines in the world. Chambertin was the favorite wine of Napoleon, whose armies lugged cases of it on his campaign in Egypt and to the disastrous winter in Russia. The greatness of French wines is rooted in such humble villages throughout France.

Welcome sign at Hargrave

Similarly, Cutchogue, the center of Long Island's fledgling wine industry, does not have the appearance of being the capital of much of anything, except rural normalcy. One stop light designates the main intersection, where a few stores cluster. There is a drug store, a bank and a clean, white Presbyterian church. Sidewalks extend only one block on either side of the intersection, then give way to lawns and fields that border the main road. It is the home of many of the East End's vineyards, and its reputation as the hub of eastern United States wine-making is growing rapidly.

The wine industry has a major significance for Long Island's East End. That part of the Island, particularly the land stretching out to the northeast of Riverhead, the North Fork, is a traditional agricultural area. And, typical of such areas in the eastern United States, it has been threatened by the seemingly inevitable encroachment of housing developments and strip malls. To the East End farmer, the financial rewards of growing cauliflower and potatoes have, at best, remained static over the years, while the offers of the developers continually escalate. Growing grapes and making wine is one of the few agricultural activities that can compete economically with conventional development—if the wine is good enough.

Baroness Philippine de Rothschild, the principal of Château Mouton Rothschild, is fond of saying that "Wine making is really quite a simple business.

Only the first two hundred years are difficult." The Long Island wine region is now over 25 years old, but when a single experiment takes at least a year and the number of variables affecting a wine is almost infinite, it is not surprising that the process of discovery takes decades, even centuries. The winemakers of Long Island are still in the process of discovering the potential for fine wine buried in the soils of the East End.

You can learn about Long Island wines in restaurants or with the help of your local wine shop, but the most enjoyable and instructive path is by visiting the vineyards themselves, and by meeting the people who grow the grapes and make the wine. Wine is an eloquent expression of a particular locality by creative people who share a culture. We are fortunate that in this field we can get close to the creative process.

All of the Long Island wineries welcome visitors. Despite their growing fame, these are mostly family enterprises, and the visitor is welcomed with a friendly hospitality. One often meets the owner or winemaker, particularly if the vineyard is visited during the week. Most wineries depend on sales from their tasting rooms for a significant fraction of their income. There are often special bottlings that can only be bought at the winery; a late harvest wine produced in very small quantities, for example. Many of the wineries provide informative tours and most host special events such as concerts or barbecues, proudly accompanied by their wines.

We should say something about how we describe and evaluate wines. Both describing wines and evaluating them are no simple matters, as the human vocabulary is very weak in matters of taste and smell. Although there have been attempts to develop a consistent vocabulary of wine tastes, those systems ultimately depend on analogies and comparisons. Wines are termed "thin," "lively" or "voluptuous," for example, or they are said to be buttery or to have the flavor of raspberries. We will use such terms in describing specific wines, but we recognize that there are no absolutes in matters of taste.

We have avoided the common practice of giving wines numerical ratings, for two reasons. First we believe that wine quality is a multi-dimensional affair. Mostly, wine is drunk just before or with a meal, and the real question is, "What is appropriate," not, "What has the highest rating on a scale of fifty to one hundred." A rack of lamb candlelight dinner deserves quite a different wine than an al fresco picnic lunch by the sea. Long Island produces wines suitable for both occasions, and almost any other you can imagine. Individual taste, the nature of the occasion, the season, the company and one's budget all play a part in deciding what is appropriate.

The second reason is that any ranking would soon be obsolete. It is an unfortunate fact of Long Island wine life that the outstanding wines of a given vintage are sold out quickly. Thus, rather than evaluating specific wines of specific vintages, we have attempted to characterize the winemaker's approach and to describe the distinguishing characteristics of each vineyard's wines.

We hope that our descriptions of wines and vineyards will entice you to discover the Long Island Wine Region for yourself. The full story is only hinted at in this book. Fortunately, it is still out there to be told by the grape growers, the vintners, the restaurateurs and, especially, by the wines themselves.

Chapter II
Climate, Soil, Grapes and Wine

"Wines express their source with exquisite definition. They allow us to eavesdrop on the murmurings of the Earth."
—Matt Kramer
Making Sense of Wine

What is it that produces a great wine? This question has perplexed wine makers and consumers for thousands of years, and it remains the subject of hot debate. On the surface, the question has a simple answer. Producing a fine wine requires the correct combination of three factors: the physical environment, the grape varieties used, and the techniques of vine management and wine making. Reaching consensus on the correct combination of these factors, of course, is the trick to the riddle. There is no magic formula for a great wine, but thousands of years of experimentation and discovery have provided some guidance for the modern winemaker.

LONG ISLAND CLIMATE AND SOIL

Nature's role in creating a fine wine is captured in part by the notion of *terroir*. There is no term in English that is equivalent to the French *terroir*, nor as richly evocative. The word encompasses all of the elements of soil, landscape and climate at a specific location. These elements determine the quality of the grapes grown there and, ultimately, the quality of the wines made from them. In France, terroir is usually used to describe the characteristics of a particular wine growing commune, a specific property within the commune, or even a small parcel of land (a *cru* in Burgundy.) The emphasis in the French usage is on the chemical and physical properties of the land, and the microorganisms of the soil (terroir also means soil or earth in French). But the concept also includes the tilt and exposure of the land, the distribution of rainfall and sun over the year and all of the other vagaries of microclimate. For example, is the soil porous or does it retain moisture? Is it rich in calcium, iron and other minerals? Is the site less prone to hail or heavy rain than another property? Does it have an advantageous southern exposure?

vines at Pindar

These and other questions identify the factors that are viewed as significant in giving one wine-producing zone, or an estate within that zone, an edge

7

in making great wines. What is more, terroir is the major factor in determining a wine's personality: the characteristics that distinguish it from wines made elsewhere, even when the same grape types are used. Wines made from pinot noir grapes cultivated in Chambertin are unmistakenly different from those made from the same variety in Oregon or the Russian River Valley in Sonoma. Not necessarily better, but clearly different.

It is also undeniable that differences in aroma and flavor may exist between wines vinified in an identical manner from the same grape clones in two parcels only a few meters apart. Those differences in nuance are persistent and characteristic. They spell the difference, for example, between the wines from the vineyards of Perrières and Charmes in Meursault, or between those of Monprivato and Villero in Castiglione Falleto. In Bordeaux, such fine distinctions of terroir are often blurred by the tendency of Châteaux winemakers to blend vats from grapes grown in different vineyard plots.

What defines Long Island's terroir? The characteristic that is most obvious is its climate: the sunniest in New York State, with temperatures moderated by the surrounding waters. This climate is quite similar to that of the Médoc in Bordeaux and also not very different from that of Burgundy. Indeed, climatologically, Long Island is much closer to these French wine regions than it is to California, and that fact gives the first clue to the general style of Long Island's wines.

Traditionally, particularly in France, soils are considered a key, and by some *the* key, to a wine's special character. Where do the mineral, flinty scents come from in the wines of Graves, Pouilly Fumé or Barolo, if not from the soils?

Some properties of the soil, such as drainage, can be of great importance in rainy areas such as Bordeaux and Long Island, while insignificant in areas with dry, hot summers such as California and Australia. When the roots of a vine absorb too much water, the flavors of the grapes are diluted and the skins can burst. Leaf growth is stimulated, grape clusters are shaded, ripening can be delayed and problems of fungal infection and rot become more pronounced. In the Long Island circumstance, adequate drainage is more of an issue than soil fertility, as are variations in vineyard slope, and the depth and extent of vine roots.

The nature of the soils of Long Island was determined some ten thousand years ago when, at the end of the last ice age, a retreating glacier sculpted Long Island. It is thought that the two forks of the Island's East End correspond to the two final advances of the Wisconsin glaciation. On the South Fork one can still see round depressions, or kettle holes, that are the imprints of slowly melting blocks of glacial ice plowed under the surface by the glacial mass. The glacier thoughtfully left behind a soil that is virtually ideal for growing grapes in the current Long Island climate. It is sandy and coarse, with some loam, and is largely permeable to water. The driest soils tend to be on the tops of the hillocks that undulate gently across the landscape, and the wettest tend to be in the low lying areas. Different grapes have their favorite locales. Cabernet Sauvignon, for example, prefers the dryer knolls, while Merlot prefers the flat lands.

Because soil constituents can play a role in wine flavor, terroir can have a time dimension. Early on, some critics of Long Island wines claimed they could taste the residual flavors from the cauliflowers that were grown in the fields before vines were planted. In many of the great vineyards of Europe, yeast-laden, fermented skins have been returned to the soil year after year for centuries. The gradual build-up of nutrients from that special form of soil fertilization, and the symbiotic relationship with the wild yeasts that inhabit the soil, all contribute to the untold nuances of aroma in the wines of Burgundy and elsewhere. On Long Island, for the most part, winemakers rely on cultivated strains of commercial yeast that are trouble free, but which may restrict the palette of aromas. Over time, as Long Island vines have grown older, and as their roots have penetrated deeper into the earth, the relationships between vine and soil have changed. By now, many vines have reached maturity, while others are being planted each year. The relationships between vine and soil are complex and will continue to evolve.

The issue of terroir exists on various geographical scales, from the regional to the very local. On Long Island, because of the lack of hills and the geological uniformity of the soils, there are not the sharp vineyard-to-vineyard variations that exist in Burgundy or in Piedmont. There are, however, variations on two other scales. First, the topsoil that covers gravel and sand tends to be thin and subject to local erosion. Thus, in the lower areas of a given vineyard, the soil can be significantly richer and heavier than the higher, well drained, eroded soils. Several winemakers have by now identified the areas that tend to produce the most desirable grapes (which generally are the better drained areas) and selectively use those grapes for their premier wines.

Second, there are significant differences between the North and South Forks that lead to two designated regions, or Appellations: "North Fork of Long Island" and "The Hamptons, Long Island." The wine-producing region of the South Fork is an oblong of land roughly twenty miles long and seven miles wide. The Atlantic Ocean to the south takes the edge off winter temperatures and cools down the summer with ocean breezes. The predominant winds, however, are westerlies that pass over the main body of Long Island and a small stretch of Great Peconic Bay.

9

Long Island Sound at Macari

The North Fork is a narrow finger pointing in a more northerly direction than the South Fork, almost exactly to the northeast. At its thickest it is a mere five miles across. Long Island Sound lies to the west and north; the Peconic Bay to the south. If you stand on a beach half way out the North Fork and look due west, into the direction of the prevailing wind, you look straight down the Sound. The line of sight would hit land around the New York-Connecticut boundary, some fifty miles away. In contrast with the main body of Long Island, over which the South Fork breezes blow, the Sound in winter is a heat source. The North Fork's winds are preferentially warmed, yielding a slight, but significant temperature advantage.

A good measure of temperature as it affects the growing of grapes is the number of "growing-degree days." This is a measure of the extent to which temperatures exceed fifty degrees Fahrenheit over time. On the North Fork that number is about 3,000 while it is around 2,500 on the South Fork. More critical, perhaps, is the fact that on the North Fork, the last spring frost occurs around the beginning of April, while in the Hamptons it can be as much as three weeks later.

There are also significant differences of soil between the two Forks. Although soil composition can vary markedly within distances of ten or twenty feet, the soils of the South Fork tend to be richer, while those on the North Fork tend to be more gravelly and better drained. The combination of all of these differences would appear to give the North Fork a decided edge, particularly for red grapes. This impression gained some credence when the South Fork's two initial undertakings in the 1980's, Le Rêve and Bridgehamton Winery, became conspicuous failures. Both had started as serious ventures, with verve and panache, and their demise did not bode well for the appellation.

Fortunately there were good reasons not to be too pessimistic. Bridgehampton Winery chose a low-lying, poorly drained site whose disadvantages were too much to overcome, in spite of owner Lyle Greenfield's creative energy. For its part, Le Rêve was handicapped by an ambitious and headstrong owner who seemed to understand neither the culture nor the economics of making wine.

Before harvest at Pindar

After harvest at Pindar

Before he started his South Fork winery, Christian Wolffer was encouraged by the experiences of his immediate Sagaponack neighbor Alan Stillman, who was consistently producing reliable chardonnays in his own private vineyard. When Herodotus Damianos of Pindar purchased Le Rêve, renamed Southampton Winery by the bank that took over the then bankrupt property, he called it Duck Walk. Though grapes were and still are bought from the North Fork, new vineyards were planted and are now thriving. These accomplishments showed that the South Fork failures were evidence of local and individual shortcomings, not regional ones. Later Channing Daughters joined the company of Duck Walk and Wolffer and it too has cultivated grapes successfully. It can be argued, in fact, the the South Fork confers some distinct advantages to grape growing. The cooler climate, relative to the North Fork requires that the grapes hang on the vine for a longer time but this generally means that sugars and acids come into balance slowly but more evenly and the tannins tend to be milder.

Grapes grown in Nassau County at the Banfi estate are another matter, since the vineyards are inland and in a distinctive microclimate. Moreover, vinification takes place at a winery in upper New York State.

Terroir, of course, has no meaning independent of the grape varieties that are planted. We now turn to the specific grapes that have been found to be most eloquent in expressing the Long Island terroir.

THE GRAPES OF LONG ISLAND

While there are recurrent discussions about the relative merits of the various species of grape vines, one species, Vitis vinifera, has all but conquered the wine world. Vinifera vines, encompassing some originating in East Asia, were brought to Europe from the area of the Caspian Sea and they form the basis of virtually all the wines of Europe, certainly the finest ones.

The American continent was endowed with a much wider variety of native grape species. Concord and niagra, for example, belong to the Vitis labrusca species and historically formed the basis of many American wines. They have a characteristic flavor, however, often referred to as "foxy," that most people find undesirable in a wine. They could never produce wines of the distinction and subtlety of a cabernet sauvignon or chardonnay. Unfortunately, some regions of the United States, including upstate New York, are simply too cold to produce wines from many vinifera varieties on a reliable basis. Thus, tremendous efforts have been made to develop hybrids that combine vinifera qualities with labrusca hardiness. The so-called French hybrids were developed as early as the 1880s in France, not so much for their cold-hardiness as for their resistance to the phylloxera louse. Even the hybrids, however, are no match for true vinifera varieties when noble wines are the objective.

Except for one ill-fated attempt to grow and sell seyval blanc, one of the finest French hybrids, grape growers on Long Island have concentrated on vinifera grapes. In fact, many of the most notable wines produced on Long Island are varietals; that is they are made predominantly from a single vinifera grape variety. Federal law requires that a wine labeled with a varietal name contain at least seventy-five percent that grape. The other category of notable wines constitutes the red blends, in many cases using the classic grape varieties of Bordeaux.

In the following pages we introduce the principal grape varieties used on Long Island. As we shall see, these grapes tie the eastern end of Long Island to the great wine producing areas of the world.

THE WHITES

Chardonnay

Most Long Island winemakers – and wine lovers – would agree that chardonnay is the premier Long Island white wine. The fact that chardonnay has also been this country's fashionable white wine over recent years suggests that market demand may play a role in the priority given to it. However, the fact remains that the soils and climate of the region appear to be extraordinarily well suited to chardonnay; proof can be found in the bottles of almost every Long Island winemaker.

Macari Vineyard flowering vine

Until very recently, the chardonnay grape was thought to be a close relative of the noble pinot noir. The truth of the matter is quite different. Apparently once upon a time a randy pinot descended from his castle and sought his pleasure among the common folk. In 1999 grape experts were shocked to learn that DNA analysis proved that chardonnay is in fact a cross between the princely pinot and a lowly (i.e. non-vinifera) grape called gouais blanc. Perhaps because of that mixed lineage, chardonnay is a relatively easy grape to grow. It has been called forgiving, for it grows vigorously, has relatively high yield and is not damaged by Long Island's winter temperatures. Its major fault is that it can be fooled by a late winter warm spell into an early budding which is then susceptible to spring frosts.

In any event, chardonnay was a logical bet for Long Island. The chardonnay grape forms the basis of some of the finest white wines of France. The white wines of Burgundy, for example, from Chablis at the region's northern tip, down through Montrachet in the Côte de Beaune, to Pouilly Fuissé in Southern Burgundy, are made almost exclusively from the chardonnay grape. In Champagne, chardonnay is usually combined with pinot noir and/or pinot meunier to produce that region's sparkling delights. Some excellent champagne is also made from pure chardonnay, and is usually labelled Blanc de Blanc (white wine from white grapes.) Vineyards from Chile to South Africa to Australia, not to mention California, now produce excellent chardonnays to meet an apparently insatiable world market. It is even said that far more "chardonnay" is drunk each year than is produced from chardonnay grapes.

Although there is a great variety of wines produced throughout France with the chardonnay grape, it is useful to distinguish the clean, tart, crisp wines characteristic of Chablis from the heavier, richer wines of Meursault or Montrachet. The differences are complex, but one crucial influence is the more common use of oak barrels for aging of the southern Burgundy wines. Chardonnay's varietal flavor is often muted, and the kind of oak, and its method of use, will have a strong influence on the character of the resulting wine.

13

Indeed, one of the reasons winemakers like to make chardonnay is that there are several factors under their control that can be used to craft the final product. Among these are the clonal variety used, harvesting conditions, temperature of the first fermentation, whether or not a secondary (malolactic) fermentation is used and whether or not, and what kind of, oak barrels are used. Practices have evolved over time on Long Island. For example, in the late 1990s it was determined that the widely used Davis (California) chardonnay clone was inferior in flavor to the Burgundian "Dijon" clone.

One of the first serious efforts to make a Burgundy-style chardonnay in the U. S. was by James Zellerbach at Hanzell Vineyards in California in the 1950s. Zellerbach was scrupulous not only in managing his vines, but also in using Limousin oak barrels for aging his wines. The success of the Hanzell chardonnays was an important ingredient in establishing a California style of chardonnay—rich, nutty, buttery, with vanilla tones created by time spent in oak. Indeed, oak flavors predominate in many California chardonnays to a much larger degree than in the white Burgundies that are their inspiration.

On Long Island, a wide range of chardonnays is being produced. Although most winemakers use a malolactic fermentation (a secondary fermentation) to produce a rounder and softer wine, a few do not, preferring a brighter flavor. Several vineyards produce two chardonnays. One may be designated as a Reserve or Estate Reserve which tends more to the California or Southern Burgundy style. The other is usually a straight chardonnay, fermented in stainless steel tanks, and which may have little or no oak aging. This produces a brighter, lighter wine more reminiscent of a Chablis. The best grapes may also be used in the Reserve, and there may be other differences as well. You can be sure that the Reserve will be more expensive. It is always interesting to taste different chardonnays made by the same winemaker in the same year, since the effects of specific choices are revealed. You may even prefer the standard variant over the fancier wine. It is a question of taste.

Sauvignon Blanc

There is considerable dispute about second place in the Long Island white wine hierarchy. This may reflect the market, for the American public is far less unanimous when considering anything beyond chardonnay. It also reflects differences in taste and preference between the owners and winemakers themselves, but the proponents of sauvignon blanc can make a strong case.

The sauvignon blanc grape is grown across a broad band of Europe extending from Bordeaux on the Atlantic coast, through France and Northern

Italy and into Yugoslavia, Bulgaria and Romania. The grape is also the basis of varietals in South Africa, Australia and South America. It is Sancerre, however, a village clustered on a young breast of a hill above a bend in the Loire river that is the center of sauvignon blanc culture. It is there that the wines epitomize the fresh, clean character of the grape. The town may well have been the birthplace of sauvignon blanc, for it is said that the monks of a nearby abbey isolated the grape by careful, time-consuming selection in the Middle Ages.

In other parts of Europe sauvignon blanc is known by a variety of names. On the bank of the Loire opposite Sancerre is the village of Pouilly-sur-Loire. There the local name for the grape is blanc fumé, and the wine produced is the universally appreciated Pouilly-Fumé. In Bordeaux the sauvignon blanc grape teams with semillon to produce an extraordinary range of white wines from unctuously sweet Sauternes, such as Château d'Yquem, to the rich, but dry whites of the Graves region.

In the United States, Robert Mondavi elevated sauvignon blanc from a grape misused in mediocre wines to the front rank by adding care and oak aging to the winemaking process. He called the resulting wines Fumé Blanc. There is now a wide range of sauvignon-based wines produced in California, unfortunately with no consistent stylistic difference between those called Fumé Blanc and those labeled Sauvignon Blanc. On Long Island, Alex and Louisa Hargrave produced ingratiating sauvignon blancs, using the name Blanc Fumé for their wine in homage to the enchanting wines of the Loire Valley.

At their purest, sauvignon blanc wines are full of fresh, tart aroma, sometimes with a whiff of peaches. They are zesty, refreshing wines with the best having an additional flinty or smoky (fumé) flavor and moderate depth. They are wines to be drunk well-chilled and young, within a couple of years of harvest.

Sauvignon blanc takes naturally to the Long Island climate. However, particularly in a wet summer, it is prone to attack by botrytis and black rot. Its Achilles' heel is its vigorous vegetative growth that produces an herbaceous flavors and as it continues through the end of the summer, makes the vine susceptible to winter injury. Vineyard managers tend to use both restricted trellis systems and severe hedging to control that growth.

In addition to Palmer and Bidwell, the winery on Long Island that has had the most attentive – and successful – devotion to the variety has been Jamesport Vineyards. In recent years, Channing Daughters and Macari have also produced fine examples of Long Island sauvignon blanc.

Gewürztraminer

Winemakers are generally an optimistic breed. They have to be or they would not survive the vicissitudes of the business. But even they can be discouraged. The odd hurricane that ravages a promising harvest can do it. So can gewürztraminer. Many Long Island vintners produce ingratiating, flavorful gewürztraminers, but have great trouble selling them. The vintners say it is a public relations problem: the public just doesn't understand the wine. Furthermore, they do not know how to pronounce it, and that is even more inhibiting. For the record, put the accent on "würz" and pronounce the "w" like a "v."

Although the gewürztraminer grape is widely planted, it is in Alsace in France that it achieves its recognized identity. Gewürztraminer vies with riesling for the place of honor in that region, and if gewürztraminer takes second place, it is because of its own versatility. Gewürz means spice in German, and fine examples of the wine are always imbued with a flowery bouquet and a spiciness that accounts for its name. However, the wine can range from dry to sweet, and from light to high in alcohol, depending on the heat of the summer and the method of vinification. The classic Alsatian gewürztraminer, however, is an enchanting combination of sweet, rose-scented aromas and a dry but complex taste.

On Long Island, Patricia and Peter Lenz, the founders of The Lenz Winery made the first serious attempt to produce gewürztraminer. Pat, a highly regarded chef, wanted to produce a wine that would complement the flavorful cuisine of the United States Southwest. They aimed at a fragrant but dry Alsatian style, and it is that approach that predominates among Long Island vintners today.

In principal, it should be easier to produce a classical gewürztraminer (and riesling) on Long Island than in California. The hotter West Coast climate tends to increase sugars and lower acids with the result being a loss of varietal character and structure in the wine. The major hazard in growing the grape on Long Island is that the vines are subject to winter damage unless their natural, vigorous growth habits are carefully constrained in the latter part of the growing season.

Long Island gewürztraminers are extremely likeable wines. Perhaps a little difficult to pair with food, but marvelous with a picnic, before dinner or with a curry or other spicy fare. The Lenz Winery continues to produce fine gewürztraminer, as does Palmer and Bedell Cellars.

Riesling

Riesling is the grape of the finest wines of Germany, those produced along the Rhine and Mosel rivers. The grapes are sometimes called white or

Johannisberg riesling and, in the hands of German winemakers, produce a marvelous spectrum of wines. On Long Island it is a controversial grape. Richard Olsen-Harbich, who apprenticed under Herman Wiemer, a master riesling maker, was a staunch advocate of the variety during his tenure as winemaker at the now defunct Bridgehampton Winery and then at Jamesport. Others say that riesling is just not suited to Long Island's warm, wet summers. Although the vines are not fazed by Long Island winters, the grapes are prone to bunch rot during all too characteristic warm, wet periods. Some riesling vines planted in the early eighties were even torn out at the end of the decade.

Part of the difficulty in selling riesling is the impression of American wine drinkers, an impression based on an earlier California, rather than the German, version of the wine. The grape produces its greatest wines—crisp with beautiful, fruity aromas—in cooler climates. The heat of a California summer can wilt the structure of riesling and produce a flabby, uninteresting wine. While there are now some fine rieslings produced in California, particularly of the sweeter, late harvest variety, it is the high volume, mediocre wines that have given riesling a bad name in this country. The winemakers of Washington, Oregon and upper New York State, however, are producing rieslings of interest and integrity more in keeping with the German standards.

Whether Long Island, with its warm summers, can produce rieslings of the highest quality on a consistent basis remains to be seen despite encouraging evidence from Channing Daughters, Peconic Bay and particularly Jamesport Vineyards. If the Long Island rieslings have thus far not had the depth of their prototypes, they generally have been fresh and crisp wines with lovely floral bouquets characteristic of the variety. Recently, Paumanok Vineyards has produced both a dry riesling and a popular, semi-sweet version.

Long Island winemakers have, when conditions were favorable, also produced worthy late harvest rieslings. The riesling grape is naturally high in acid and can be left on the vine much longer than other varieties to allow the sugars to concentrate. The first late harvest riesling produced on Long Island was made by Richard Olsen-Harbich at Bridgehampton Winery. Nice examples have also been produced by Bidwell, Bedell Cellars and Paumanok.

Pinot Blanc

Pinot blanc, a clone of the red pinot noir, is a popular varietal in Alsace, northern Italy and recently Oregon. The leaf clusters are sometimes difficult to distinguish from chardonnay, and some early plantings on Long Island thought to be chardonnay turned out to be pinot blanc. Turning disappointment to their

17

advantage, at least one winery, on discovering pinot blanc in a newly acquired vineyard of "chardonnay," adapted their vinification techniques to the imposter. While pinot blanc generally can not produce wines of the depth and complexity of chardonnay, they are often clean, delightfully drinkable – and affordable wines. In recent years Palmer has made a successful specialty of the variety and the grape constitutes a major planting at Lieb Cellars.

Viognier

Every once in a while, in a mysterious way, a particular grape variety will emerge from obscurity and become widely, if not wildly, popular. That seems to be happening with viognier. Twenty years ago the world's total planting of the grape amounted to some 80 acres, and its esoteric repute rested entirely on the small output of white wines of Condrieu and Château Grillet in the Northern Rhône. Grillet, with its mere 8.4 acres is unique in constituting its own tiny appelation. The luster of these wines was burnished by a series of renowned chefs who had restaurants in the neighborhood, starting with the great Fernand Point at La Pyramide in Vienne. As a white grape, viognier is highly unusual in that it is sanctioned for use in the high quality red wines of the region's Côte Rôtie.

With its extremely small yields and fickle ripening, viognier is not easy to grow. It is also difficult to vinify. But its unique sensory appeal provides suffi-cient incentives to winemakers to overcome those hurdles. In Robert Parker's words, viognier's irresistible charm resides in its "seductive perfume of honey-suckle, peaches, and apricots, and the lush, rich fruitiness found in such a dry, concentrated wine." Its distinctiveness from any other grape grown in France has inspired theories of exotic origins, and historians now believe that Greek sailors brought the viognier grape up the Rhône Valley in the fifth or sixth century B.C.

In the 1980's viognier started to be planted on an experimental basis in the southern Rhône. It then started to appear in the southwest of France, and plantings increased for the first time in centuries in the Condrieu region. At the same time, California caught the viognier bug and soon thereafter viognier fever started to be detected on Long Island. Pindar, Martha Clara, Macari, and Bedell are all producing enticing versions.

Other *Whites*

There are a few other white grapes that have been grown successfully on Long Island and there is talk of several more. Chenin blanc produces a diversity of wines around the world. While it is most abundantly planted in South Africa, the best known versions of chenin blanc are those from the Loire regions of

Vouvray, Saumur and Anjou. At its best, it exhibits a floral bouquet and a texture that Rabelais associated with taffeta. For some years Paumanok Vineyard has produced a fine example.

At least in Italian restaurants, pinot grigio is as ubiquitous as chardonnay. Another mutation of the prolific pinot noir, pinot gris, as the grape is known in France, is a favored grape in Alsace (where it is also known as Tokay d'Alsace). It is also widely planted in Germany where it is sometimes called ruländer. Why not a Long Island Pinot Grigio? Duck Walk has 14 acres planted to the grape and Channing Daughters also has a significant planting.

THE REDS

Merlot

The name merlot is sometimes associated with merle, the French word for blackbird, and the bird's ravenous taste for the grape gives the connection some credence. The emergence of merlot as Long Island's premier red wine grape, and the public's taste for it, is a bit surprising. Cabernet sauvignon would have been a more obvious choice because of its commercial appeal, and some maintain that cabernet will win out in the long term. In the meanwhile, merlot's ascendancy is an encouraging indication that the Long Island terroir is being allowed to direct the outcome of varietal experimentation in the region.

 Merlot is a major constituent of many of the great wines of Bordeaux. In fact, in the greater Bordeaux region there is almost twice as much land planted in merlot than in cabernet sauvignon. Many of the wines of Pomerol contain merlot as the primary constituent. Château Pétrus, the district's most famous wine, and some would say Bordeaux's greatest, is usually made with one hundred percent merlot grapes. In many of the vineyards of St. Emilion, where it is usually blended with cabernet franc, merlot also predominates.

Beyond France, the merlot grape is grown widely throughout Europe, and seems to express itself best in a relatively northern climate. It produces fine wine in northern Italy, Switzerland, Yugoslavia and Hungary. In recent years it has been the fastest expanding variety in California.

The adjective that most often characterizes the quality given to a wine by the merlot grape is softness. Wines made purely from merlot mature quickly and can be enjoyed young, but, the great Pomerols not withstanding, they can be somewhat one-dimensional. While merlots typically have generous fruit flavors, they often lack depth and complexity. After a typical summer, merlot grapes will contain a high sugar level, but much lower tannins than cabernet sauvignon. On Long Island, it is thus common to blend some cabernet sauvignon (ten to twenty percent) to give a merlot wine more backbone and complexity.

One of the greatest risks in growing merlot results from one of the grape's otherwise desirable characteristics: its vigorous growth habits. After a cold winter, merlot is raring to go in spring. An early warm spell can trigger the budding process, and if temperatures then return to below freezing, the buds can be killed. A related problem is coulure, a failure of flowers to develop. The vine is also susceptible to winter damage. Cold winters of 1984 and 1987 in Bordeaux killed forty- to fifty-year-old vines by the thousands. Nonetheless, in the Long Island climate, merlot attains an early, full ripeness and can be picked at whatever point the winemaker considers ideal.

With plantings totaling almost 400 acres, merlot is the most widely planted red grape on Long Island. Only chardonnay is more widespread, and as with chardonnay, virtually all of the Long Island vineyards make a merlot varietal wine. In good years, such as 1993, '95 and '97, several vineyards may decide to bottle a special merlot, often called a Reserve, as well as their standard bottling. Over the years, Bedell Cellar's opulent Reserve Merlot has been the touchstone of Long Island merlots but in any year there may be literally dozens of worthwhile merlots produced in the region. In 1997, the stature of merlot on Long Island was reinforced by the decision of Paul Pontallier, the General Manager at Château Margaux, to participate in a new winery, Raphael, whose principal wine will be based on this grape variety.

Cabernet Sauvignon

Bordeaux has an aura of nobility. With its venerable chateaux and its roots extending back to the first century A.D., it all but defines the culture of wine. Despite the sale of prominent chateaux to British and Japanese conglomerates, the region still bespeaks a natural aristocracy, in touch with the soil and with the finer things in life. From the days of Thomas Jefferson, American connoisseurs have taken the wines of Bordeaux as their standard of vinicultural quality. Although several grape varieties are used in Bordeaux wines, the most notable and characteristic is cabernet sauvignon.

Winemakers call it "Cab," and their affection for the grape is not surprising. It has all the qualities of a perfect friend. It has a strong and vivacious personality, is hale and hearty, and is reliable. Unlike pinot noir, for example, the trusty cabernet sauvignon flavors emerge under a wide range of growing conditions. Admittedly, like some of the most interesting older people, in its youth cabernet sauvignon can be objectionable: aggressive and overconfident. These personality traits derive from relatively large pips and thick skins, which produce naturally strong tannins. The sharp edges of cabernet's personality become smoothed by age, however, and in the best cabernet sauvignon wines a marvelous medley of flavors emerges over time; flavors of spice, black current and other fruits, that complement the vanilla tones imparted by the casks in which the wine is fermented and stored.

In its youth pure cabernet can be so awkward and take so long to mature that in most Bordeaux wines it is blended with softer grape varieties such as cabernet franc or merlot. In response to impatient market forces, winemaking techniques are also being adjusted to produce cabernets that are approachable earlier in life.

Although it can be grown under a wide range of conditions, cabernet sauvignon requires a high accumulation of heat during the summer to bring out its best. Some Bordeaux summers fall short and other grapes such as cabernet franc, whose quality varies less with temperature, are used as a partial replacement. Sugar must often be added in the fermentation process. On Long Island, while the summer temperatures are generally higher than in Bordeaux, many summers are not quite long enough to produce perfectly ripened grapes. Long Island winters are also more severe, and cabernet sauvignon vines can suffer as a result.

Most wineries on the Island produce a "cab", often adding ten to twenty percent merlot to soften the wine and make it accessible earlier. Among the wineries consistently making cabernets of superior quality are Palmer, Pellegrini, Lenz, Gristina, Duck Walk and Paumanok. The Hargraves used the grape in their original planting. While some of their early bottlings were uneven, others, such as the 1980 Vintner's Signature Cabernet Sauvignon, have demonstrated that Long Island Cabernets can acquire Bordeaux-like complexity and integration with bottle age of over a decade.

Pinot Noir

Many wine lovers and several winemakers on Long Island would agree with Alec Waugh when he wrote: "At the age of twenty I believed that the first duty of a wine was to be red, the second that it should be Burgundy. During forty years I have lost faith in much, but not in that." To many, the highest accomplishments of the winemaking art are the great red wines of Burgundy: Chambertin, La Tâche, Clos de Vougeot, Richebourg and their brethren.

The pinot noir grape is the basis for all of these wines. No grape, however, is as elusive and difficult. In part this is because it exists in so many slight genetic variants and is so sensitive to growing conditions. Jancis Robinson describes pinot noir as "a minx of a vine...an exasperating variety for growers, winemakers and wine drinkers alike. It leads us a terrible dance, tantalizing with an occasional glimpse of the riches in store for those who persevere, yet obstinately refusing to be tamed." Over 200 clones of pinot noir have been identified in Burgundy alone. Two dozen varieties may contribute to a single wine. Some would say that this clonal variety is one of the secrets of the subtle complexity of the great Burgundies.

Pinot noir leads a double life, for in addition to producing celestial red wines, it is also a primary constituent of the great sparkling white wines of Champagne. In that role it is often blended with some combination of chardonnay, pinot meunier or pinot blanc. Unless a pink sparkling wine is desired, the skins are removed from the juice immediately after the black grapes are crushed.

On Long Island, quality red wines from pinot noir are more of a dream than a reality. A major problem is the Long Island climate. The close packing of the grapes in the cluster makes pinot noir highly susceptible to bunch rot in such a damp climate. It was one of the original grape varieties planted by the Hargraves and at Lenz Winery. They both make pinot noir wines from time to time. Gristina Vineyards also produces small amounts of pinot noir from their grapes. Others, such as Palmer Vineyards, have used pinot noir to make rosé wines by allowing the naturally white juice to have only brief contact with the skins. Both Pindar and Lenz have used pinot noir in sparkling wines. In 1998, Russell McCall, a newcomer to Long Island if not to the wine business, planted 11 acres of pinot noir in Cutchogue.

Whether Long Island ever produces a notable pinot noir remains to be determined, but we doubt whether the winemakers will ever give up the search. Pinot noir devotees will just have to be patient. After all, by the time Louis IV became devoted to their wines, the Burgundians had been experimenting with the best combination of clonal variety, location and winemaking technique for well over a thousand years.

Cabernet Franc

If, as a youngster, you had an annoyingly successful, smart and popular older brother or sister, you know how cabernet franc must feel. As the younger sister to cabernet sauvignon, cabernet franc is often not given the respect she deserves. Why should cabernet sauvignon get all the publicity? It is true that the older brother is more assertive and bold (older brothers are always full of acid and tannin) but the younger sister has some exceptional qualities of her own.

Bird netting over grapes at Lenz

Macari Vineyard, Mattituck NY

Cornfield on the North Fork

Images of the East End

*Bedell
Cellars*

*Grapes at
Gristina Vineyard*

*Ripe cabernet
sauvignon grapes*

Images of the East End

*Laurel
Post Office*

*Gazebo in
Pellegrini
Vineyards*

*Waterside
view near
Greenport*

Kip Bedell

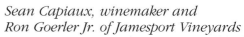
Sean Capiaux, winemaker and
Ron Goerler Jr. of Jamesport Vineyards

Tom Drozd, winemaker
at Palmer Vineyards

Herodotus Damianos with sons
Jason and Alex at Duck Walk

Her voice is softer and she wears delicate perfumes. As a youngster she is much more approachable. In some ways, beneath the surface, she is stronger than her older brother. For example, she gets through a cold winter in much better shape. The delight, though, is that when the brother and sister play together constructively, they bring out each other's best.

While less prevalent than thirty years ago, cabernet franc is still one of the major grape varieties of Bordeaux. It is usually a minor (ten to twenty percent) partner, but in St. Emilion it often plays a major role. Château Cheval Blanc, often referred to as the quintessential St. Emilion wine, is normally about two thirds cabernet franc. Like merlot, it is used to soften the hard edges of cabernet sauvignon, and contributes its own complexity and floral bouquet. There is sometimes a spicy or briary flavor to cabernet franc wines; Robert Parker detects a "weedy, olive-like aroma," while Jancis Robinson is reminded of the aroma of pencil shavings. This is sounding less and less like something one would be inclined to drink.

Nevertheless, in the Loire region cabernet franc is a favored red wine grape, being used for the bold reds of Bourgueil and Chinon, for example. That region's best rosés, particularly from Anjou, are also made from this flexible variety. In northern Italy, the grape has been at least as popular as its more famous brother, presumably because it produces a wine that is ready to drink sooner after harvest. In California, cabernet franc is widely used, usually as a minor partner to its better-known sibling, but increasingly as a pure varietal wine.

Cabernet franc is being given the chance to stand on its own on Long Island by several wineries including Palmer, Pindar, Paumanok, and Hargrave; Schneider Vineyards built its early and esteemed reputation on the variety. In most cases Long Island cabernet francs include some cabernet sauvignon to create a firmer structure. There is often a race to see whether cabernet sauvignon will ripen before the fall frosts arrive. Cab franc always accomodates by ripening at least a couple of weeks earlier.

The wines of Long Island have contributed to cabernet franc's self-esteem. On top of that, now that it has been shown that cabernet sauvignon is in fact a descendent of cabernet franc (in a cross with sauvignon blanc), cab franc has lost all sense of inferiority.

Other Reds

Long Island seems to be a propitious environment for many varieties of red grapes and experimentation with new varieties is more active now than it has ever been. Some plantings, such as those of malbec and petit verdot are designed for use as components of Bordeaux-style blends and are found at several properties including Pindar, Macari, Pellegrini and Raphael. Others are forming the bases of varietal wines, such as syrah at Pindar and Macari, Duck Walk's unusual pinot meunier, and Channing Daughter's dolcetto.

Other Wines

By a wide margin, most of the wine produced on Long Island is varietal, based on one of the grape varieties discussed above. There are other notable wines, however, that will reward the visitor. These non-varietal or blended wines fall into several categories.

The first is a premium quality red wine, blended from a mix of grapes, as is done by the great châteaux of Bordeaux. Indeed, some would maintain that the next leap forward in the quality and reputation of Long Island wines will be based on these refined blends. The grapes are usually fermented separately and then, after several months of barrel aging, are combined in the proportions that the winemaker feels is the most propitious. Pindar Vineyards, under the guidance of Dimitri Tchelistcheff, produced one of the earliest and most successful Bordeaux-style blended wines based on cabernet sauvignon. Pindar's Mythology, incorporating merlot, cabernet franc, petit verdot and, in some years, malbec, is only produced when the owner feels the quality of the grapes is sufficiently high. Long Island's wine industry doesn't lack a competitive spirit. In 1993, using only three letters, Alex Hargrave entered the Bordeaux-style contest with characteristic condescension and wit. By calling their deep and complex Bordeaux-styled blend, Q.E.D (Quod Erat Demonstrandum) he implied that only with their entry was it proven that a wine worthy of Bordeaux could be produced on Long Island. He reinforced the claim with a price tag of $45 a bottle. In recent years, other notable Bordeaux-style blends have been produced by Pellegrini (Encore) Paumonok (Assemblage), Bedell (Cupola) and Ternhaven (Claret d'Alvah).

While the Bordeaux-style blends are near the top of the pyramid in terms of quality and price, many wineries also produce non-vintage red and white blends that are remarkably good-drinking wines at prices often well below $10.00 a bottle. Pindar makes something of a specialty of such wines and their Winter White, at $8.00 a bottle, is the region's best selling wine. Blush and rosé wines, spanning a wide range of prices and levels of sweetness, appeal to a wide range of tastes. Some of these low-priced wines use grapes from other regions, but in those cases will not carry the "North Fork of Long Island" or "Hamptons, Long Island " designation on their labels.

Sparkling wines constitute a further category of non-varietal wines produced on Long Island. The controversy over what can and cannot be called Champagne has been raging for decades over dinner tables and in the international courts. The French consider that only sparkling wine from specified regions of the province called Champagne (made from certain kinds of grapes according to specified techniques) should be able to bear that magic name. We accept that position, not in support of French chauvinism, but in admiration of the quality of Champagne from Champagne. Wines that are made using the traditional method, in which the second-

ary fermentation occurs in the bottle, are referred to as méthode champenoise sparkling wines. An alternative and less expensive method, developed in 1907 by Eugene Charmat, carries out the secondary fermentation in tanks. These wines are referred to as Charmat or bulk process sparkling wines. Sparkling wines can be made from a variety of grapes. Those made only from white grapes, often chardonnay, are called Blanc de Blanc.

An increasing number of Long Island wineries have been attracted to the making of sparkling wine, all in the traditional méthode champenoise. Both Lenz Winery and Pindar Vineyards use a combination of red and white grapes as does Wolffer/Sagpond in their Christian Wölffer Cuvé. Pindar has also made a pink sparkling wine and an unusual Cuvée Rare sparkling wine from pinot meunier grapes. Pugliese Vineyards makes a notable Blanc de Blanc.

Pat Pugliese painting sparkling wine bottles

Sweet dessert wines constitute yet another tempting specialty of many Long Island vineyards. Several years ago Kip Bedell noticed that the fungus, Botrytis cinerea, had attacked a portion of his chardonnay vineyard. Taking his cue from the sweet wines of Sauterne, where botrytis is allowed to dry out and intensify the sugar in grapes at the end of their ripening, Kip produced an intense, deeply sweet, late harvest wine; a highly unusual form of chardonnay. He and others now sometimes produce an "eis" wine, using artificial freezing of the grapes after harvest to concentrate the juices. The process is based on a natural phenomenon pushed to its risky extreme in some German wines, where the grapes are traditionally harvested in December and even January (the Dreikönigswein.) Among other wineries producing notable late harvest wines are

Pellegrini (their Finale), Duck Walk (Aphrodite), Paumanok and Peconic Bay. Port-style wines are produced by several wineries including Pindar, Osprey's Dominion, and Pugliese.

Long Island's winemakers are a highly skilled, creative lot and even this long list of Long Island wines doesn't do justice to their inventiveness. The visitor shouldn't be surprised to encounter an experimental zinfandel, a "nouveau" wine from last fall's harvest, or even a wine made from raspberries. Generally these wines are only available at the vineyard, and, in these days of increasing uniformity in winemaking methods, they bring a special pleasure to the wine lover.

FROM GRAPES TO WINE

Before there were wineries on Long Island, there must have been visions of vines clinging to trellises in long rows of verdant foliage, of attractive oak casks neatly stacked in a cool cellar and of bins upon bins of bottles with pretty labels: the ultimate expression of a proprietor's whimsy. A vast chasm stretches between these visions and their attainment, however. Years of nurturing and waiting, of financial investments that may never become profitable, of doubt and uncertainty, and of learning on the job await the new vineyard management. Despite new evidence of winemaking in Mesopotamia five millennia ago, there is still no foolproof prescription for a successful vineyard. The Long Island winemaker must make countless decisions throughout the seasons, but the net result of those decisions does not appear in the bottle for some years.

The first critical decision leading to a successful winery is the selection of the vineyard site. This is arguably the most important factor in determining the quality of the grapes and the yield of a vine. Our earlier discussion pointed out that different fates await grapes that grow in sunny elevated sites with good drainage, as opposed to those that grow in the more poorly drained and cooler areas. Water and cold air tend to collect wherever the landscape is depressed. This can lead to an excessive proliferation of vines during the growing season and to an increased risk of killing frosts in winter. Moreover, deposits of silt and non-porous materials from an adjacent hill can build up in a gully. This exacerbates the poor drainage of bottom sites. On the other hand, if a slope is too steep, the water available to a vine planted there is drastically reduced.

One Long Island vineyard owner was plagued for over ten years with an ill-chosen site, before he tore out acres of vines and moved elsewhere. Perhaps it took the unfortunate owner so long to admit the site's inadequacy because of year to year shifts in weather. Even a poor site can produce decent wine in favorable years. Perhaps it was the natural reluctance to give up on a vineyard that has cost so many dollars and taken so much effort to develop. Whatever the case, as Alex Hargrave once said, "The most creative act is where the winemaker plants his grapes."

Another consideration in choosing a site are the flocks of migratory birds that move across Long Island. If the vineyard is surrounded by woods and shrubs—good roosting areas—the risk of bird damage is increased. Especially troublesome has been the voracious starling. Charming in small numbers, these migratory birds become a dark, Hitchcockian menace as they sweep down in flocks of thousands, just as the grapes are reaching their ripe perfection. They can devour or spoil acres of ripe grapes in a matter of hours.

Long Island vineyard owners have tried all kinds of weapons in this battle: propane cannons, four-wheel, all-terrain vehicles, miles of shiny mylar tape, hawks, party balloons, and netting. Gristina Vineyards once tried what is perhaps the most unusual defense. For a while, a young man by the name of Jeff Morgan worked for Gristina as marketing and sales director. Jeff was also a classical and jazz musician who wielded

Netting the vines

his saxophone in the annual war against the attacking flocks. He found that be-bop and certain kinds of free jazz, "free and fast arpeggiated lines," were particularly noisome to Gristina's feathered enemies.

In 1989 and 1990 the bird problem seemed to be getting worse and worse. Many vineyards, including Gristina, concluded that the only solution was to put netting over the entire vineyard during periods of bird migration. By then Jeff Morgan had moved on to become a respected wine reporter, but some say that on still and moonless nights, they can hear echoes of plaintive saxophone rambles floating through the Gristina vineyard.

A second critical decision, closely related to the issue of site selection, is the choice of grape variety. That choice has become increasingly easy over the years as experience has been gained on how different varietals have fared in the vineyard, and how the wines fared in the bottle. Some, like cabernet sauvignon, exhibit vigorous growth and so are best planted on lighter, more elevated soils, while others, such as chardonnay, adapt to the drainage conditions found on a plateau. By now, any newcomer to the wine-making fraternity can draw on the accumulated wisdom of the other vineyard managers and winemakers. However, key uncertainties still remain, many of which revolve around marketing issues. In five years will there be a market for another chardonnay? Can we charge enough for a sparkling wine to make it worthwhile?

Hidden enemies of the vineyard manager are the fungi that attack the roots of the vines. Others are more apparent, such as the many forms of molds and mites that attack the grapes themselves. Given its damp climate, Long Island would not be successful in growing vinifera grapes were it not for chemical sprays to prevent rot. However, the possible degradation of the underground aquifers that are infiltrated by these pesticides is a concern. Needless to say, the federal Environmental Protection Agency provides regulations that are monitored regularly to protect fragile groundwater supplies, but the concern remains and today there is increasing interest in using natural predators to control the unwanted pests.

Perhaps the answer lies in alternate strategies for vineyard management, such as new trellising methods, or more careful canopy management that allows sunshine and cooling breezes to offset the harm done by humidity. The goal of canopy management is to expose the fruit to sunlight to enhance maturation and reduce the incidence of mildew. However, even though the exposed grapes become riper and fruitier, an excess of sun can result in raisiny and slightly cooked grapes and therefore the amount of foliage removed from the canopy must be judged with care.

A related problem is the choice of rootstock. Experiences in California indicate a revival of Phylloxera, a tiny louse that attacks the root system and withers the vine. This scourge affects a substantial fraction of the acreage planted in California and necessitates replanting with rootstock resistant to the pest. Long Islanders are keeping a wary eye on this possible affliction which, to date, does not appear to have penetrated the region.

One enemy that is practically unique to Long Island is the hurricane. It is an enemy of huge power for which there are no defenses, and it tends to attack at the vineyards' most vulnerable period, just before harvest. In late August of 1991, for example, Hurricane Bob roared through Long Island, with the eye passing over the eastern tip. While some vineyards were essentially unaffected, others, such as Jamesport Vineyards, suffered sufficient damage that they decided to pick their chardonnay before the bruised grapes spoiled on the vine. The Hargraves made the same decision, not because of physical damage, but because the spray carried on the post-storm winds left slight salt deposits on the grapes that they feared would lead to damage. Hurricanes evidently breed a kind of resourcefulness that is special to Long Island winemakers.

Following site selection the future viticulturist must prepare the land for planting by removing weeds and shrubs as well as trees, large rocks, and other obstructions, prior to plowing the field. Soil pH must be adjusted to a neutral value of about six by liming, since most of the uncultivated soils on the North Fork are fairly acidic.

Then the trellis is installed, with its vine supporting poles and wires. Next, the young vines are planted in rows running generally north-south to enhance sun exposure and reduce shading in the leaf canopy. At sufficient maturity, anywhere from three to four years after planting, the first grapes are harvested.

Conventional wisdom has it that only mature vines, whose roots have penetrated deep into the soil, and whose vigor of foliage and shoots is limited by age, can make a great wine. This is so because the less prolific vine can concentrate its growth on the few remaining grape clusters that now benefit from the attention they receive. However, the noted British wine authority, Clive Coates, affirms that although it is no doubt true that older vineyards, thirty to fifty years old perhaps, produce superior wine, there are exceptions, such as the 1961 Pétrus. That legendary wine was made from very young vines. He argues that a five year old vine produces as small a number of grapes as an old vine does. Thereafter the vines become more exuberant and need to be tamed.

New vines at Macari

There are annual vineyard rituals that are familiar to grape growers the world around. During the late winter or early spring, when the vines have shed their foliage and lie dormant, the Long Island growers emerge to prune back the straggly and tangled mass to permit just a few pre-nascent buds to remain on the branches. At the same time, some of the slender canes of the vines are reposi-

29

tioned and tied to the trellis wires. Later in the spring, after bud-break and when

the first clusters of fruit have set, any excessive leaf growth is pruned away, the vines are hedged and unwanted shoots at the base of the trunk are "suckered" or clipped away. During the summer a grower may remove some of the grape clusters in an attempt to concentrate the vines' vigor on the remaining crop. This reduces the yield at harvest, of course, but it also augments the color and extract of the grapes that remain. It is a trade-off between quality and quantity.

Quite possibly the most significant advances in Long Island viticulture in recent years has been to move from a high to low wire vine support and to increase vine density. The older high wire trellising allowed

Pruning of the vines

the vines to sprawl about in disarray making them harder to prune but, more importantly, some clusters would be over-exposed to sunlight while others were excessively shaded leading to uneven ripening. As for vine density, the increase has been achieved by planting between existing rows or, in the case of new vineyard sites, by planting rows closer together, with more vines per row. The desired result has been to reduce the yield per vine. However, since there are now more vines the total yield per acre remains comparable to what it was before. In effect, though the yield is the same, quality has increased.

Finally, clonal selection has become of more interest lately as the growers have become more attuned to the local conditions of Long Island climate and soil and can begin to be less concerned with the choice of grapes to plant and to focus on which clone of those grapes to adopt. More clonal variety is available to growers today than in previous years and it is generally agreed that clonal selection may be as significant a factor in wine quality as any other.

As much as possible the grower attempts to expose the fruit to sunlight and cleansing breezes. The goal is to obtain healthy and mature grape berries before harvest. After veraison, when the grapes take on their pigment—usually in August—the sugar levels begin to increase and the acidity starts to drop as the fruit ripens. For most grape varietals there is an optimum level of acid and sugar that cannot always be achieved in Long Island, especially in a growing season beset by too much rainfall, cloudy days and cool temperatures. Some growers try to offset this by picking late, during the usually more favorable autumn weather, and by practicing severe crop thinning during the summer. Ultimately, it is the experience and commitment of the grower whose care in the vineyard determines the quality of the wine that goes into the bottle. Each year brings new climatic conditions to reckon with, and the grower copes with it by a combination of vigilance and hopeful expectancy, not to say prayers to Dionysian gods.

Harvest usually begins in mid to late September and may continue into October, depending on the season and the grape variety (some ripen earlier). The prudent grower will examine each vine before picking and will drop all clusters of grapes that show signs of spoilage and immaturity, leaving on the vine the ripest and healthiest bunches.

At harvest time some of the most agonizing decisions must be made. The early-ripening grape varieties, such as chardonnay, achieve the desired balance between sugar and acid content by early September and can be picked at a deliberate pace. However, a few days of unexpected rain will upset the balance and dilute the grapes' intensity of flavor. For others, such as cabernet sauvignon, few summers seem long enough, and the vineyard manager will attempt to leave the grapes on the vine as long as possible to benefit from the last warm, sunny days of fall. Grape tannins, incidentally, tend to become more supple with increased exposure since the indi-

Harvesting the grapes

vidual tannin molecules link together and get larger (polymerize) as the grapes ripen and these longer molecules do not pucker our palate as much. It is a risky gamble, however. A deep killing frost can sneak in, or a hurricane can roar by to destroy whole vineyards of precious grapes. Picking too early may result in lean and herbaceous wines but picking too late can mean deteriorated grapes, and an opportunity missed on the other side of caution. It is a decision to which the winemaker, the vineyard manager, and the owner each brings his own expertise, but which must finally be made by the owner. According to Richard Olsen-Harbich, winemaker at Raphael Vineyards, timing a harvest and controlling yields are the two most significant decisions facing a winemaker.

If the decision of when to pick is sometimes preceded by sleepless

nights, it is always followed by days of intense work that leave little time for sleep. When the time has come to harvest on Long Island, more often than not a mechanical harvester will rumble through the lanes between the vines, prying the grapes loose. In some instances the removal of grape clusters is done by hand by a team of pickers. This is time consuming and is certainly the more expensive way to harvest, but, according to some, it is the only way to select grapes. Hand sorting reduces the chance of picking up unwanted debris and leaves, or under-ripe or moldy grape bunches. It also handles the vine itself more gently. It is the way harvesting is still done at the celebrated estates of Bordeaux, and at many of the front rank wine properties throughout Europe. Yet the advocates of mechanical harvesting claim that little or no harm is done to the vines, and that grapes arriving at the winery are indistinguishable from those obtained by the more arduous hand picking method. On

grape harvester at work

Long Island both procedures are practiced and the jury is still out.

As the vines get older they lose their vigor, and eventually, after twenty five or more years, some fraction of older vines must be replanted. This hasn't happened on Long Island as yet, but replacement of dead or diseased vines is not an uncommon occurrence even now. New vines can be grafted to existing root stocks, or the entire plant may need to be taken up, and a new vine planted.

Most Long Island wineries are equipped with mechanical devices called crusher-stemmers that, true to their word, crush the arriving batches of whole grapes to release the sugary pulp within, and separate the grape berry from stems and leaves. The crushed red wine grapes flow into stainless steel tanks in which the fermentation takes place. Fermentation is a magical time when the sugar in the juice is transformed into alcohol in the presence of certain species of yeasts. The activity begins a few hours after the grape juice enters the tanks and can last several days until all, or virtually all, the sugar has been converted. Large quantities of heat are released, as well as carbon dioxide that escapes through the top of the tank. One can hear the bubbling and sizzling, and a beguiling odor emerges.

Pressing the chardonnay

Long Island vintners generally use cultivated yeasts purchased from laboratories which they then inoculate into the grape juice. Although these yeasts are selected to ensure trouble-free fermentations, a few winemakers are experimenting with a mixture of yeasts, including some natural strains that appear in the wild. It is known that many of the flavors and aromas in a wine are the result of the specific action of yeasts on the fermenting juice. Different yeasts can enhance some aromas while reducing others, thereby allowing the winemaker to enlarge the color palette of the wine. This is a technique to be used with caution, however, since certain wild yeasts can give the wine unpleasant odors, and may inhibit the positive action of other yeasts, even shutting down a fermentation prematurely.

In the middle of the last century, the scientist Louis Pasteur gave the first rudimentary explanation of fermentation by implicating micro-organisms as catalysts. Significantly, lack of that knowledge did not impede previous generations in their winemaking. What happens during fermentation requires little intervention except for an occasional nudge and some corrective action here and there. For example, if the temperature in the tank is too high or low (fermentation works properly only within a certain range) the winemaker can correct it by cooling the tanks or heating the cellar. On Long Island, as elsewhere around the world, a few winemakers have invested in temperature controlled fermentation tanks to reduce the element of chance.

While fermentation proceeds, the juice is pumped over the cap of solid matter that has floated to the top in order to extract more color and flavor. When it is complete, the tanks are sealed to prevent spoilage of the wine by acetic bacteria in the air that convert the alcohol into vinegar. For certain wines, mostly reds, a second fermentation is allowed to take place in which other strains of bacteria act to convert the tart malic acids in the wine into the softer lactic acid, while also reducing overall acidity. This malolactic fermentation is a desirable change in that it can make a wine more supple and less biting. It also generates a by-product called diacetyl that confers a buttery feel to the wine. Malolactic fermentation is routinely practiced on Long Island for many of the merlot and cabernet sauvignon wines and for some chardonnays.

After fermentation has been completed, the detritus in the tank is allowed

Stainless tanks at Duck Walk Vineyard

to settle out, and the clear liquid is pumped to a new tank or, depending on the wine, into wood barrels where the aging process begins. Before that occurs, the pumice at the bottom of the tank, consisting largely of grape skins, is gently pressed to squeeze out the juice that is trapped in the mass. This is carried out in another mechanical device appropriately called a presser. On Long Island this press wine is usually, though not always, added to the other juice to add more body and color. This is done with some care in order to avoid a certain harshness of flavor that comes from the tannin in the skins and pits. For white wines this pressing is done at the beginning, not long after crushing, to avoid long skin contact that would color the wine too deeply.

When, in the judgement of the winemaker, the new wine has reposed sufficiently in its tank or barrel, it is ready to be filtered of impurities and clarified prior to bottling. The wines destined for aging may be given more time in wood than others in order to allow certain gradual, chemical reactions to take place. With time, complexity increases. Oak, in particular, has a notable effect on the flavor of the wine and, used with moderation, enhances the fruit aromas of the grapes. The barrel staves are generally toasted by the supplier, to a lesser or greater degree, and this charring can impart certain smoky vanillin

34

flavors to the finished wine. At present most wood barrels on Long Island are made from French oak. However, in any given cellar an assortment of other barrels may be found, including American white oak. These wood nuances can be exaggerated, however, and, although wood aging is commonplace on Long Island, it is one place where the wine-maker's good sense must come into play.

Another critical activity is that of blending. Wines from different parts of a vineyard are sometimes fermented separate-ly, as are the different varietals. After aging is completed, wines from the individual vats are tasted to determine which, if any, should be blended together, and in what propor-tions. The idea is that the whole may be bet-ter than its constituent parts, and it may be that a blend of cabernet sauvignon, cabernet franc and merlot is a more harmonious enti-ty than a wine made from any one of the

Winemaker Ryan Leeman washing filters at Paumanok Vineyards

grapes alone. One varietal lends tannic backbone and firmness, another supple-ness and seductive aromas, and a third provides certain spicy, exotic highlights, just as baritone, tenor and alto voices enrich each other while harmonizing in a choral group. Sometimes a solo voice is more compelling, however, and so it is that a wine made mainly from a single grape type may convey a richness and texture that is satisfying by itself.

Once the wine has been pumped into sterile bottles and corked, another machine-regulated task, the labels are put on and the wines stored in cool facili-ties. The job of promotion, sales, and distribution can now begin.

We have stated that the most significant changes for Long Island wine have been the recent changes in viticulture which, to a greater or lesser degree, have been adopted by all the vineyards. Changes that take place in the cellars after harvest, on the other hand, have been more idiosyncratic and less systemat-ic, reflecting primarily the personality and training of the winemaker. There are many small choices available for fine tuning a wine after the grapes have been brought in and crushed. The sum total of these small "tweakings," as the wine-maker Eric Fry calls them, determine the overall style of the wine. For example,

35

instead of pumping the grape juice over the cap in a fermentation tank with a hose, at least one winemaker opts to gently splash the juice to minimize friction and increase aeration. Another winemaker has constructed a device to hoist the tanks of finished wine directly over the bottling apparatus so that the wine can flow by gravity smoothly into the bottles, a less violent procedure than siphoning. Still other winemakers now routinely subject the newly crushed grapes in a fermentation tank to a sharply reduced temperature without the addition of yeasts for several days. This process, called cold maceration, extracts water soluble compounds from the grapes, enhancing fruit aromas and color while extracting mild tannins. Thereafter, the temperature is increased and fermentation proceeds as usual. Finally, one winemaker partially barrel ferments the red wines. This process, though a standard procedure for the more opulently styled Reserve Chardonnays, is an uncommon treatment for red grapes but it does appear to impart a creamier texture to the wine.

From a marketing point of view, wines made from blends of grapes are more problematic for Long Island vintners, since it is not clear what to call them. The public recognizes the name cabernet sauvignon, but it might shun a hybrid product with which it is unfamiliar. The red wines of Bordeaux are in fact blends, but the consumer has come to know them by the name of the estate or the commune in which the grapes are grown, rather than by the varietal name. Eventually the North Fork appellation may shift a wine's repute away from grape type towards place of origin.

Some Long Island wineries are fortunate in having several accomplished artisans who daily exercise their skill in a multitude of tasks, from vineyard management to nursing the wine into being in the cellar. The same technical experts may counsel several wineries, not unlike the midwifes of earlier times. Sometimes the winemaker is the owner, a double jeopardy where judgment in matters large and small shape the final product and may give the wine a competitive edge over a similar wine made by another producer. It is one of the delights of the consumer to recognize the shades of difference between wineries and to give the palm in each vintage to the more striking wine.

LONG ISLAND VINTAGES, 1993-1999

Most wines from vintages older than 1993 are mostly memories though a few bottles may still repose in private cellars or in the reserve bins of a few wineries. Should you be able to latch on to a wine from an older vintage it is likely to be fragile and not in peak form, except for some red wines from 1988, unquestionably the best vintage on Long Island prior to 1993. A few red wines from 1990 are also excellent and quite drinkable today though they are the exception and not the rule.

1993 Warm and dry growing season, with early budding providing small yields of very ripe and concentrated fruit. An excellent vintage.

1994 Dry weather conditions early in the summer followed by a moderately warm summer. Some good to very good wines were made that year.

1995 A hot and dry growing season that persisted into autumn leading to a substantial crop of fully mature and concentrated grapes. This is another excellent vintage that may have a slight edge over 1993.

1996 The growing season was cool and slightly wet. A moderate to good vintage, especially for white wines.

1997 A wonderful spring and summer that was warm but not excessively so. The good weather extended into autumn with below average rainfall. An excellent vintage of concentrated and elegant wines.

1998 Growing conditions were almost, if not quite, identical to those in 1997 leading to wines that are nearly as good. A very good to excellent vintage.

1999 A warm and dry growing season that promised to be a repeat of 1997 until drenching rains from tropical storm Floyd in September partially diluted the crop. The growers that picked late, taking advantage of the sunny days of late autumn turned in wines that range from good to very good. Overall the vintage is likely to surpass 1996 in quality.

Snow at Gristina

Chapter III
The Historical Legacy

"...we must endeavor to make everything we want within ourselves, and have as little intercourse as possible with Europe in its present demoralized state. Wine being one of the earliest luxuries in which we indulge ourselves, it is desirable that it should be made here, and we have every soil, aspect and climate of the best wine countries."
—Thomas Jefferson, 1811

There are few commercial activities in the modern world in which history plays a larger role than in winemaking. The fabric of winemaking on Long Island, youthful and dynamic as it is, incorporates strands from many parts of the world and past eras. The soils themselves, crucial to the quality of the grape, contain echoes of their history: the great workings of the Wisconsin ice sheet that lay them down at the end of the last ice age; the crops that for many hundreds of years were grown in them by native Americans and their European successors.

The vines that grow so robustly in Long Island's soil have ancient lineages as well. Their core genetic structure probably evolved in the Transcaucasus area south of the Black Sea, but their specific characteristics result from their nurture by ancient Greeks, Etruscans, Romans and Gauls, as well as the Cistercian monks of medieval Burgundy and centuries of vineyardists in Bordeaux, Alsace and the other great wine regions of Europe.

There are some novel vineyard and vinification practices being used on Long Island. But often an innovation is merely a new juxtaposition of traditional techniques: a vinification technique typical of Germany, for example, being used for grapes traditionally grown in Bordeaux. If they visited a modern Long Island winery, Thomas Jefferson or Dom Pérignon, after tramping through the vineyard, ducking into the cellar, and asking a few incisive questions, would understand the system completely. They might even have a helpful suggestion or two.

The paraphernalia of wine consumption also participate in a lengthy historic tradition. Modern wineglasses would appear dull compared to their first century Roman predecessors. In the eighteenth century, the cork-stopped bottle evolved, much in the same shape as we know it today. At the same time, fortu-

Grange Hall

nately, some unknown genius invented the corkscrew, that indispensable device that allows us to unlock ancient legacies and pour the sunshine of a summer past into our glass.

A PERSISTENT RIVALRY

The history of winegrowing in America begins with the earliest European settlers who brought a love of wine with them from England, France, Spain, Portugal and Italy. The story has as one of its dominant themes the rivalry between native American grapes and the imported vinifera varieties. Despite an abundance of wild grapes and countless attempts in virtually all the colonies, no one seemed able to make acceptable wine from the native varieties. They ripened with too little sugar, too high acid levels and a "foxy" taste that most people found objectionable. There were always a few proud advocates of the native varieties, however. Referring to the Catawba grape, John Adlum, a viticulturist who died in 1836, declared, "In bringing this grape into public notice I have rendered my country a greater service than I could have done had I paid off the national debt." Of course, in those days the national debt didn't amount to much either. A greater contribution of Adlum was his early advocacy of the practice of grafting foreign vines onto American rootstocks.

Attempts to grow wine grapes on imported vines were even more discouraging. Time and time again American wine lovers, including George Washington and Thomas Jefferson, expended prodigious efforts to import and grow European grape varieties, only to see their vineyards die away after a few promising harvests due to local diseases and pests. Around 1740, an accident of nature was recognized by an observant horticulturist to be a possible solution to this frustrating puzzle. In that year, James Alexander, gardener to the son of William Penn discovered an accidental hybrid, a cross between a native vine and an imported vinifera growing on the banks of the Schuylkill river near an abandoned vineyard of European grapes. The Alexander grape become the first of many successful French-American hybrids. Despite some success of the hybrids, American growers continued to import European varieties in a frustrating attempt to emulate European wines. New York State was no exception to the early settlers' desire to grow wine grapes. Vines were planted up the Hudson River from New York City to New Paltz as early as 1677 by French Huguenot settlers.

EARLY VINES ON LONG ISLAND

There is a theory that the first Europeans to set foot on Long Island were

Bristol fishermen who, in the late 15th Century, sailed west from their familiar fishing grounds off Iceland. Certainly, Verrazano sailed along the south-east coast of the Island in 1524. The English colonists, as they spread south and west from New England in the 1630s started to explore the coast and bays of the eastern end of Long Island, including the "Great River" between the forks. From their settlement in New Amsterdam, the Dutch pushed east. Both became acquisitively interested in the East End because it was there that indians produced the most striking and valuable wampum in the country. Wampum crafted from the shells of Peconic Bay was a preferred currency even for the fur traders in the mid-west.

A few hardy individuals settled the east end of Long Island in the 1630s. A land agent for the Earl of Sterling, James Farrett was living on the North Fork when, in 1639, the engineer-adventurer Lion Gardiner acquired his island from the Montauk Indians and changed its name from the Isle of Wight to Gardiner's Island. It was in 1640 that significant settlement took place on eastern Long Island. On the South Fork adventurous farmers came ashore from the bay side around Southampton and East Hampton. The North Fork was also settled in that year by a party led by the Reverend John Youngs from the New Haven Colony. They called their new settlement Southold, in deference to Southwold on the east coast of England, that Youngs, his family, and some of his congregation had left only three years before.

When the settlers arrived, Indians had been living on Long Island, or at least fishing and hunting there, for at least 4000 years. Bones from graves on the South Fork have been dated to 1290 B.C. In the 17th century the predominant Indians, called Corchaugs by the English, were woodland Algonquins. Weakened by war and disease, they acquiesced in the Europeans' occupation of the land, putting their names on deeds that were foreign in language and concept.

The settlers divided the land into large tracts, built houses and churches, and planted corn, wheat and barley. Some of their original fields now yield cabernet sauvignon and chardonnay grapes. Others still produce corn or potatoes and there is more than one farming family on the East End who can trace its lineage back to those original settlers. One is the family of John Wickham, who played a central role in the history of wines on Long Island.

The East End gradually became a flourishing agricultural region with grapes being a prominent crop. There are intriguing stories of a Moses "The Frenchman" Fournier growing grapes in Cutchogue on the North Fork by the end of the 17th century with the aid of the local Indians. Some claim that he even grafted French varieties onto native vines. A history of Cutchogue by Wayland

Jefferson mentions that his "great vineyards were an outstanding feature of the town" in the early eighteenth century. More authoritatively documented is the fact that a Francis Fournier and his family lived in Southhold in the 1750s. Said to be "very successful in setting out the grape and making it grow," Fournier and his brother-in-law, Joshua Clark, planted some 4700 vines between them in the 1760s.

At about the same period, at the other end of Long Island, the Prince family was establishing its reputation as nurserymen. As the fourth generation in that trade, William Robert Prince was the most notable precursor of Long Island's current viniculturists. In the early 19th century, Prince operated the Linnæan Botanic Garden in Flushing (in Queens County), popularly known as Prince Nurseries. In 1829, he published his important discovery that a spray of a lime-sulfur mixture was effective against oidium, a common mildew. Unfortunately, that treatment was not effective against black rot and downy mildew, which eventually destroyed his vinifera vines. Those blights would not be conquered until 1885 with the discovery of Bordeaux mixture, a combination of copper sulfate and lime. In 1830 Prince published *A Treatise on the Vine* which contained a "history of vinegrowing since Noah", instructions on vineyard practices and a description of 280 varieties of grapes, many of them vinifera. The treatise was by far the most authoritative work on the subject published to that date in this country. Prince also made wine from several grape varieties, but they were apparently not for public sale.

While the most prominent, Prince was not the only serious wine grape grower on Long Island in the nineteenth century. One of the most successful hybrid grapes he sold, the Isabella, was developed on the Island by Colonel George Gibbs, who named it after his wife. In the early days of the century, Alphonse Loubat cultivated a vineyard of some forty acres along what is now the Brooklyn waterfront, and André Parmentier conducted extensive vinicultural experiments at the corner of Jamaica and Flatbush Avenues in Brooklyn. Both of their efforts were based on vinifera varieties, however, and were doomed to failure.

One of the most controversial chapters in the history of American wine-making concerns the origins of Zinfandel, sometimes called California's mystery grape. A popular account identifies Zinfandel as one of the grapes brought to this country from Hungary in 1852 by the legendary Count Agoston Haraszthy, who is known as the "Father of California Viticulture." A fatal flaw in that account is that there is no mention of a Zinfandel-like grape in Hungarian ampelographies of the time, nor has there been any since.

Another problem with the theory of the 1852 introduction of Zinfandel to this country is that William Prince was growing Zinfandel at least as early as 1830. Prince advertised "Black Zinfardel" [sic] for sale in his catalog of that year. It was probably also grown near Boston in greenhouses around that time. Recently, it was determined that zinfandel is closely related to the Croatian vinifera grape, mali plavač which has been grown in Croatia for over 1000 years. Mali plavač seems also to be the ancestor of the Italian primitivo. How it made its way to New England and to Prince's nursery remains a mystery.

Further out on Long Island, at least by the 1870s, there was a successful vineyard and winery on the western shore of Stony Brook Harbor in what is now

After a nineteenth century Long Island wine label (courtesy of Mrs. Prescott B. Huntington)

the Village of Nissequogue. According to the 1879 records of the Town of Smithtown, when Thomas Seabury sold his estate, Rassapeague, "extensive vineyards, the most complete collection of choice wine grapes in New York State," were included in the sale. The new owner, a Mr. Ruszits, built a separate building for his wine cellar, and his Rassapeague Claret was highly reputed. A few years later, when Edward Kane bought the gristmill in nearby Stony Brook, he planted a vineyard and hired "a Bohemian miller who made good wine, played the violin and sang Bohemian songs."

The early nineteenth century also saw new vineyards planted north of

New York City along the Hudson River. In 1839 a Frenchman named Jean Jaques established a vineyard and winery at Washingtonville. In the 1870s its name was changed to the Brotherhood Winery, and it continues to make wine to this day, the oldest winery in continuous operation in the country. A link was forged between that history and Long Island in 1999 when Cesar Baeza, President of Brotherhood Winery, joined with a group of Chilean investors to buy Laurel Lake Vineyard on the North Fork.

Despite their disadvantages, native American grapes, and then the French-American hybrids, were the basis for a burgeoning grape and wine industry in the far western part of New York. and in the Finger Lakes region between Pennsylvania and Lake Ontario. The driving forces behind the upper New York State wine industry in this period were often French and German immigrants fleeing political turmoil in Europe. These promising efforts, and those on Long Island were hobbled by the onset of Prohibition in 1919.

By the time Prohibition was repealed in 1933, the U.S. wine industry was in a shambles. Lucie Morton, author of *Wine Growing in Eastern America* , comments, "Wine was viewed as either too lowbrow for respectable households or so esoteric that you had to speak French in order to understand it." Over the next two decades, that gap was bridged in the eastern United States by the efforts of a few wine importers, writers and winemakers, such as Frank Schoonmaker, Philip Wagner, Charles Fournier and Konstantin Frank. Of particular importance to the story of Long Island wines is Dr. Frank, a viticulturist and enologist who was born in Russia to German parents. Frank ran a vinicultural research institute in Russia and, after the Second World War, worked for the American occupation forces in Germany on agricultural projects. Eventually, in 1951, he and his family made their way to New York, arriving there with forty-one dollars between them.

As soon as he had saved a few more dollars, earned by washing dishes, Frank headed for the nearest wine region: New York's Finger Lakes district. He was determined to make wine there from vinifera grapes, despite two centuries of evidence that that was an impossible dream. Starting in the position of an unskilled vineyard hand, he eventually persuaded Charles Fournier to back his efforts. To much shaking of heads, Frank planted riesling and gewürztraminer vines. In his 1961 vintage, Frank produced a riesling trockenbeerenauslesen that caused a sensation. Made from hand selected grapes shriveled by botrytis rot, the naturally sweet wine sold for the unprecedented price of forty-five dollars a bottle, more than Frank's net worth when he arrived in this country ten years before.

Konstantin Frank, through his demonstration that vinifera grapes could be grown in the eastern United States, through his influence on the next generation of New York winemakers, and through visits to Long Island, had a profound influence on the Island's wine future. His name will come up several times as the story of Long Island wines unfolds.

WINES ON THE EAST END

Certainly by the 1840s, wine was being produced on the South Fork. In his book on viticulture and winemaking published in Brooklyn in 1846, Alden Spooner mentions that grapes were being grown for wine in Southampton. Winemaking persisted on Long Island up through the mid-twentieth century, due mainly to the efforts of amateurs.

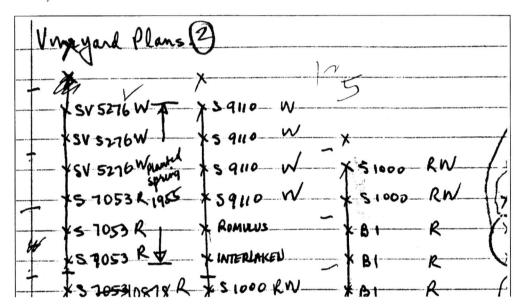

Detail from Anderson's notebook, 1953. (Courtesy R. Christian Anderson)

As farmers of other nationalities followed the English, they brought their own vinous interests with them. The Italians, in particular, often made wine either from local grapes or from grapes shipped in from California by freight car. This, for example, was how the Pugliese family (of Pugliese Vineyards) and the Petrocelli family (owners of Raphael Vineyards) got into winemaking. East End farmers, seeking to diversify their crops beyond the declining bulk staples of potatoes and cauliflowers, experimented with alternative crops. One of those farmers, John Wickham, planted table grapes, including vinifera varieties. There was also a small number of intellectual amateur winemakers scattered around the Island who made wine from their own grapes. An interesting example is

45

R. Christian Anderson from the hamlet of Brookhaven.

With his long intelligent face, hollow cheeks and beard, "Andy" Anderson's appearance is strikingly Lincolnesque. In spirit, however, he is clearly Jeffersonian. He holds a Ph.D. in Chemistry and in the mid-1950s was working at Brookhaven National Laboratory in Suffolk County. His notebooks of that period reflect their author's personality: rational, orderly, creative, humane and widely curious. The notebooks are very American in their confidence and openness to the world, but their broad scope is also very much of the eighteenth century. They could have been written at Monticello.

Some pages of the notebooks are alive with ideas for new scientific experiments, but the books are not limited to scientific ideas. There are also architectural sketches of the modern house that the Andersons were planning, along with layouts for a home garden. At first these are simple vegetable plots, then more elaborate designs including orderly arrays of flowers, vegetables and a fruit orchard. Then, in 1953, there appear notes on the characteristics of various French-American grape varieties, and the garden designs start to include vineyards.

In 1954 Anderson planted two varieties of seibel and one of seyve-villard. Soon his vineyard included close to 100 vines of five or six varieties. They were all French-American hybrid grapes, representative of a period of intensive hybridizing and experimentation that started in the 1880s in France. The stimulus in Europe for this work was the devastation of French vineyards wreaked by the phylloxera epidemic. In the United States such hybrids were seen as a solution to the vulnerability of pure European varieties to a wide range of American pests and diseases. With the chemical treatment methods available even by the 1950s, the pure French and German varieties were highly chancy in the damp climate of Long Island.

There was a second reason why Anderson chose the French-American hybrids. In the 1950s there was little interest in, and even less knowledge of, cabernet sauvignon or chardonnay. California was producing "Burgundies" and "Bordeaux" and insipid "Sauternes" which bore absolutely no resemblance to their namesakes. Seeking the grape varieties that had the best chance of producing good wine on Long Island, Anderson understandably focussed his attention on the hybrids. He pressed his first grapes in 1957. Over succeeding years, however, Anderson endured one Job-like trial after another. His troubles ranged from bunch rot to hurricanes to flocks of voracious birds. His problems were not only caused by nature. Once, his upstate supplier sent mislabeled vines to him.

Years later, Anderson confessed that, while his wine wasn't exactly bad, it was "completely undistinguished." Others have a much more favorable recollection of his wines, particularly the whites. Anderson eventually gave up his experiments, but they provided an important piece of evidence that quality wine could be produced from Long Island grapes.

JOHN WICKHAM

John Wickham, who died in 1994 at the age of 85, was a patriarch of farmers on the North Fork and is often referred to as the grandfather of Long Island's wine industry. This despite the fact that he was a teetotaler. Wickham's family has been farming on the North Fork for 330 years on land that the Corchaug Indians cultivated before them. Parts of the farmhouse date back to 1659. There was a certain Old Testament aura about John Wickham. When you shook his large hand you could feel the texture of years of handling axes, shovels, innumerable varieties of trees and plants, rocks and quantities of good soil. It was said that he went without socks in summer in order to toughen up his feet for the winter. One got the distinct feeling that his views, while expressed with courtesy and restraint, were handed down from on high and to be questioned at some unmentioned peril.

Wickham was in his senior year at Cornell training to be an engineer when his older brother died in a car crash. He took over the farm and became the most innovative and respected farmer in the region. The engineer-turned-farmer became interested in growing table grapes to sell at his farm stand in the early 1950s and wrote to the New York State Agricultural Experiment Station run by Cornell University in Geneva, New York, asking for recommendations. Cornell wrote back to say that there was not enough experience in New York State to form the basis of a recommendation, and they proposed a cooperative experiment. Wickham enthusiastically agreed and expressed particular interest in vinifera varieties. Eventually he planted some 100 varieties of grapes, about a third of which were vinifera.

Konstantin Frank, who propagated many of the vines supplied to both Wickham and Andy Anderson, made several trips to Cutchogue during the course of Wickham's grape growing experiments. The relationship between the gentlemanly, but strong willed men was not always easy. Frank, for example, was keen about a certain type of Muscat seeded table grape that was very popular in Europe. Wickham found that his farm stand customers didn't particularly like the flavor and, in any case, insisted on seedless grapes. When he heard that Wickham had torn out the Muscat vines, Dr. Frank was incensed and scolded, "It took 3,000 years to develop that grape and now you want it to be seedless!"

THE HARGRAVES

The seminal event that would eventually give birth to Long Island's modern wine industry was a visit to Wickham's farm by Alex and Louisa Hargrave in November of 1972. The Hargraves had developed their joint interest in wine in the late 1960s while they were newly married students at Harvard, Louisa an undergraduate in Chemistry, and Alex a graduate student in Chinese Studies. Wine was a natural accompaniment to food in their families. Both Alex's father and an uncle were outside directors of the Taylor Wine Company. But it was in Cambridge that they fell under the influence of the likes of Julia Child and started to cook and taste French wines seriously. Gradually, they became more and more taken with the idea of growing premium grapes, and eventually

Alex and Louisa Hargrave

making their own wine. The idea had an irresistible appeal. They could continue to pursue their intellectual interests and their interest in wine, and at the same time do something more real, more tangible, than their business-oriented families.

A visit to the West Coast in 1971 convinced Alex and Louisa of two things: that small, family-scale wineries making premium wines could be viable, and also that California was not necessarily the best place to make such wines. For one thing, land prices had already become uncomfortably high. When they returned to New York, the Hargraves sought the advice of John Tompkins, a Professor at Cornell, on where they could best grow vinifera grapes. True to the Cornell canon, Tompkins tried to persuade them to forget vinifera vines, and to grow hybrids. But when he saw they were determined, he recommended that they visit John Wickham in Cutchogue.

Before visiting Wickham, the Hargraves also gave some consideration to the Finger Lakes region where Konstantin Frank was producing wine from vinifera grapes. After visiting his vineyard in Hammondsport, however, they concluded that despite his success with riesling and gewürztraminer, even he, the magician of vinifera, could not get cabernet sauvignon to ripen adequately in that part of the State. For the Hargraves, cabernet was the measure of all things. Their next stop was Cutchogue.

Wickham was helpful and generous with his time, but did not encourage the enthusiastic young couple. He warned them of the risk of starting an entirely new type of agriculture in the area. Nonetheless, only a few months after that Thanksgiving visit to Wickham's farm, the Hargraves bought a sixty-six acre potato farm in Cutchogue from Edward Zuhoski. That same year they planted their first seventeen acres of vinifera vines, including, of course, cabernet sauvignon. Alex was 28 at the time and Louisa 25.

In conversation in the early 1990's Wickham seemed proud of the fact that the Hargraves bought land "as close as possible to our farm, no more than a quarter mile away." Driving back home one night after dinner with the Hargraves, where the talk had been charged with Alex and Louisa's enthusiasm for their new venture, Wickham's wife, Ann said, "Why John, I think you're jealous of that young couple." "I sure am." Wickham replied, "If I were twenty again I'd love to do something new and exciting like that."

John Wickham is not the only old time, God-fearing farmer in those parts. When the votes are tallied in national elections, Suffolk County is often one of the most solidly Republican in the country. Conservative rural values prevail; so also do conservative rural prejudices. The wine industry may be the saving grace of agriculture on the East End, but it sure is different from potato farming. What is more, the vineyard owners are not fifth generation farmers; they are advertising executives from New York City, or doctors from Connecticut, or retired pilots. There was the nagging suspicion among some of the locals that the newcomers were in it for the tax deduction or for some romantic winemaking make-believe.

John Wickham agreed that there was a strong potential for resentment of the nouveau farmers by those who had been growing potatoes and cauliflower for generations. An early grower and vineyard manager, David Mudd described the situation in his usual colorful fashion: "Sure, there is friction to the extent that we're the guys with the lace pants, and they're the ones with the sacks on their asses because they're going out of business. The banks won't lend them any more money." Wickham believed that it was fortunate that it was the Hargraves who came first. From the beginning, Louisa worked in the vineyards with their hired laborers, putting in days as long as any potato farmer. When the locals got to know the Hargraves and saw their dedication to their vines and to the land that supported them they were reassured. As others followed the Hargraves, there were many more stories of considerate, neighborly acts on the part of the local farmers than of conflict or resentment.

With little relevant experience and less scientific information to go on, the Hargraves hedged their bets by planting six vinifera varieties: cabernet sauvignon, pinot noir, and sauvignon blanc in 1973, followed the next year by chardonnay, merlot and riesling. With his playful intellect one could never be sure whether Alex was engaging in hyperbole when he said that in their new endeavor they was guided by the ancients. Admitting that "we didn't know what to expect," he claimed that they were following Virgil who wrote of "planting four champions." Whether they were using common sense or, as he claimed, following Columella's advice to "enquire of your neighbors," they did seek advice, particularly from John Wickham.

It is pushing things to produce wine from three-year old vines, but Alex and Louisa were eager to get into production, so in 1975 they harvested grapes for their first wine, a rosé made from cabernet sauvignon. They sold it for $3.99 a bottle. The next year, despite a hurricane that roared through the vineyards at harvest time, they managed to pick a good crop and produced their first "serious" Cabernet Sauvignon. By 1978, word was getting around about the daring young winemakers of Cutchogue. On the day that he released the '76 Cabernet, Alex was amazed to find customers waiting at the winery door when he arrived at 6:00 in the morning.

Alex and Louisa Hargrave were remarkably well suited to be the pioneers and first ambassadors of Long Island winemaking. They are a striking and engaging couple and, in a way, quintessentially American. Both of them were raised in successful American business families and are products of elite private schools. Such an environment instills a confident instinct for success. At six feet, six inches, Alex has a commanding, scholarly presence. Speaking with the colorful and confident eloquence of a college professor he could discuss regional terroir in France (and Long Island), the effects of oak or different yeasts with his most knowledgeable potential critics. The part of the public that might have been put off by Alex's somewhat distant theatricality, was charmed by Louisa's warmth and quiet earnestness. There is something old-fashioned about Louisa, who embodies a New England combination of character, independence and integrity. A certain creative irreverence is also in Louisa's genes. Her grandfather was Norman Thomas: Presbyterian minister, editor of *The Nation*, prolific author, staunch pacifist, head of the United States Socialist Party, and six times candidate for President.

While deeply American, the Hargraves' second shared culture is France. The seeds of Alex's interest in France were sown one summer while he was still at Exeter. His stay with a French farming family in the Dordogne region who made their own wine contributed to his confidence in the notion of a family-scale farm winery. Alex and Louisa's skills and interests, as well as their personalities were complementary. The vineyards were mostly Louisa's domain. It was she and her varying size crew of helpers who pruned, hedged, sprayed and harvested as dictated by joint decisions with Alex. She was also the chemist of the operation, but Alex was the winemaker. A comment once made by Louisa explained their collaboration. "I am the science," she said, "but Alex is the magic."

The Hargraves started with firm ideas about the wines they wanted to produce. At first they used conventional American, especially Californian, text-books, but soon convert-ed to French texts, partic-ularly the great work of Emile Peynaud, *Connaissance et Travail du Vin*. It turned out that there was a happy con-gruence between the French wines that most appealed to them, and the wines naturally produced by the Long Island terroir.

As the Hargraves' early wines started to appear, reactions varied greatly. Objective judge-

*Hargrave
entrance*

ment was hard to discern between the romantic's enthusiasms for the new Bordeaux, and the sophisticates' disdain for anything grown within 2000 miles of New York. But an unbiased appraisal was also difficult because the wines themselves were variable in quality, certainly between varieties and vintages, but even between different cases of the same wine. Even between different bottles from the same case. Part of that variability resulted from the Hargraves' unusual practice of bottling one barrel at a time. Critics would also detect vegetal flavors, of bell peppers or green beans, that some attributed to the cauliflower and cab-bages that had been grown in the Hargraves' fields (even fields in which only potatoes had been grown). This would be a nagging characteristic of many early Long Island wines, a trait that more logically could be attributed to the youth of the vines and to the luxuriant canopy growth that was allowed in the early years. But over time, as the vines matured and the techniques of vineyard management and winemaking settled down, it became clear that the Hargraves were making wines to be taken seriously.

Calling himself a non-interventionist winemaker, Alex defined his wine-making technique as "doing the least possible at the last possible moment." He often used cool, fresh fermentation to get a "clearer, more resonant ringing of the fruit and maintained that, "the closer you can bring your wine to ripe fruit the better your wine is going to be, now and into the future." In seeming contradiction to that objective he used oak barrels to age his larger wines, recognizing "this one great anachronism, the oak barrel" as an alternative to long term aging for wines that want to be drunk in one's lifetime.

In its early years, Hargrave Vineyard produced the classic cabernets and merlots and chardonnays that established the reference points for the region. While the pundits declared them wines to be drunk young, eventually the facts contradicted such pronouncements. While they were revelatory of the particular grapes used to make them, they were also well structured wines. The 1980 and 1985 cabernets were still lively after ten or fifteen years in the cellar. Over their 25-year history in the region, the Hargraves were also imaginative innovators. Alex's 1978 Chardonnay was arguably the first in the U. S. to be taken through complete malolactic fermentation before bottling. While initially they introduced yeasts for the secondary fermentation, they later found that the natural bacteria present in the vineyard and the cellar produced very acceptable malolactic transformation. Cabernet franc is a favorite variety of Louisa's and in 1988 they produced the region's first varietal bottling from that grape. In the same year they produced Long Island's first noteworthy pinot noir.

The Hargraves were also creative in their secondary wines. They used their Petit Château label to identify wines made from younger vines. There were also special bottlings whose labels sported art photographs or paintings from Long Island museums. When Hurricane Bob almost destroyed the 1991 vintage of Pinot Noir, and they had to work without electricity, Alex made a Hurricane Bob Candlelight Burgundy that was a charming, light, silky wine. Putting a lie to the contention that Long Island wines are too expensive, the Hargraves produced a string of extremely well crafted stainless steel-fermented white wines including pinot blancs, sauvignon blancs and the justly popular Chardonette.

If the Hargraves hadn't brought winemaking to eastern Long Island in 1973, the development of the region might well have been sparked by some other enter-prising individual. But in that case the path of that development might have been quite different. The prototype created by the Hargraves: a small, privately owned win-ery growing much of its own fruit, aiming at wine of the highest quality from the classic French vinifera varieties, profoundly affected their followers' and the world's attitudes towards the region. As though unaware of alternative models, those who came after the Hargraves, starting with the Lenzs in 1978 and Lyle Greenfield in 1979, took very much the same path. The persuasiveness of the model grew as initiatives that strayed from it failed, either because they grew the wrong grapes (at Soundview) or had a different ownership/management structure (at North Fork Winery) or simply didn't match the culture (at Le Rêve).

The earliest successful challenge to the Hargrave model was the region's largest winery, Pindar, the creation of Herodotus Damianos. The scale of production (eight times the scale of Hargrave), its product line, and particularly the audience of novice wine drinkers to which it played, defined a new paradigm for the region. What could be further from the Hargrave château canon than a wine that incorporated cranberry juice? At the same time, however, Pindar also paralleled the French/Hargrave model in a line of classic varietals. In fact, they out-Frenched the Hargraves when they crafted the region's first high quality Bordeaux blend, their erstwhile Mythology, which was supported by their own plantings of petit verdot and malbec, as well as their vineyards of cabernet sauvignon, merlot and cabernet franc.

Over time, other modest variants on the Hargrave model were attempted. In particular, various wineries essayed a much wider range of grape varieties. For example, in a thoughtful and concerted challenges to the prevailing practices, Larry Perrine at Channing Daughters on the South Fork is working with North Italian grape varieties such as pinot grigio, tocai friulano, and dolcetto. Ironically, the most complete challenge to the Long Island/French canon is occurring at the Hargrave estate itself. In October, 1999 Alex and Louisa announced that they had sold their winery to a member of the aristocratic Borghese family of Italy, for something "in the neighborhood of $4 million." This end of an era for the Long Island wine industry had a sad accompaniment in the concurrent break-up of the Hargrave's marriage. Whatever the reasons for it, to the outside world there was a dramatic poetic logic to the divorce of Alex and Louisa, for they as a couple had always been so completely identified with their Vineyard.

In his first interview with the press, Marco Borghese said that he and his American wife Ann Marie would be planting sagiovese, the primary Tuscan grape used in Chianti. Over time they would make other changes. From a larger perspective, however, all of these initiatives, by the Borgheses and others, rest comfortably within the broad pattern of high-quality wines made in small quantities from pampered vineyards of vinifera grape varieties. For now at least, the imprint of the Hargraves on the Long Island wine region appears permanent.

FAILURES

The dominant themes of the 25 year history of the Long Island wine region are strikingly positive: an increasing number of vineyards and wineries, a steady increase in wine production and quality, a solid, if hard-won, growth in reputation, more prizes, higher prices. But within this story of regional success there are also stories of individual struggle and failure. With all its surface romance, winemaking is a tough business, particularly in a new and unrecognized region. To be successful, everything has to be right: the site, the financing, the selection and management of the vines, the wine making, the weather, the marketing, and the control of expenses. Those who don't approach it as a business, or who underestimate its toughness, may not survive. There is some truth in the oft-quoted saying that "the way to make a small fortune in the wine business is to start with a large fortune."

By 1985 fifteen wineries had been started on the East End of Long Island; by the end of 1998, five of them – fully a third - had failed. In the case of the Northfork Winery, established by an out-of-state holding company in 1980, they succumbed to their own financial chicanery, a tax dodge so greedily inept that that the IRS discovered it immediately and shut them down in 1986. The mistake of Soundview Vineyards was to bet on the wrong grape variety. They produced only seyval blanc, some 8000 cases a year in the late 80s, but despite a low price there were few customers and they closed down abruptly. Soundview's owner was fond of saying that "To create a good wine is to achieve a kind of immortality." In fact, his wine was pretty good, but few on the East End remember his name.

When its vines were planted in 1979, Bridgehampton became the second winery to be established on Long Island, and the first on the South Fork. Its creative and dynamic owner, Lyle Greenfield, a highly successful advertising designer, had been beguiled by a 1978 article about the Hargraves in the *New York Times Magazine*. In Richard Olsen-Harbich, Lyle found a highly capable winemaker, as serious and quiet as Lyle was flamboyant and extroverted. Lyle created the winery's image and his winemaker filled the bottles with often superb wines. Richard recognized early the potential of cabernet franc on Long Island and his 1988 Grand Vineyard Selection Chardonnay become legendary. *The Wine Spectator* ranked it one of the world's 100 best wines that year.

But creativity, the handsomest labels in the region, expert winemaking, and endless energy were not enough. By the late 1980s it had become clear that

Palmer Vineyards at harvest time

*Ursula and Paul Lowerre with daughters
Cornelia and Lavinia of Peconic Bay Vineyards*

Bob and Joyce Pellegrini

Owner John Petrocelli with winemaker Richard Olsen-Harbich at Raphael

Christian Wolffer, owner (right), with winemaker Roman Roth and vineyard manager Richie Pisacano (left)

*Robert Entenmann with daughter,
Jacqueline, and her husband John Connolly*

Laurel Lake Vineyards

*Harold
Watts of
Ternhaven
Cellars*

Drip irrigation at Pellegrini Vineyards   *Hedging the vines at Pellegrini*

*Cellar at
Hargrave*

the Bridgehampton vineyard site was severely handicapped; drainage was poor and there were low areas that captured the cold air in the spring and fall. Acres of vines were lost to frost. Acres of land were sold off. The last vintage to be put into Bridgehampton bottles was the 1992. In 1994 Peter and Deborah Carroll, the owners of Lenz Vineyards, bought the winery equipment and inventory and acquired a lease on the buildings but gave up on the enterprise soon thereafter.

Some attributed the demise of Bridgehampton to Lyle Greenfield's lack of financial management skills. But the small-scale winery business is intrinsically marginal and it is doubtful that anyone with limited financial resources could have survived the early decision to invest in a vineyard in the wrong place.

By 1991 the South Fork seemed doomed as a wine region. At the same time that Bridgehampton was turning to vinegar, the most grandiose initiative of them all, Le Rêve, in Water Mill was filing for Chapter Eleven bankruptcy. From its beginning Le Rêve was an anomaly. If there is a characteristic image of a Long Island

Peter and Deborah Carroll

winery it is the small, family oriented enterprise aimed at producing the highest possible quality wine. The vineyards and wineries seem to have grown naturally out of the agricultural tradition, particularly of the North Fork. Their architecture, often converted potato barns, reflects a parsimonious respect for that tradition. Almost universally, there is a strong emphasis on grape quality, which means growing their own, or buying grapes from neighbors whose growing practices are carefully monitored. Although the winery owners are competitive, they also respect the community in which they are involved.

None of that for Le Rêve. As if the construction of a pompous, seventeen million dollar, copper roofed Norman-style château-winery (without benefit of a building permit) was not provocation enough, Le Rêve's seigneur, nightclub-owner Alan Barr, claimed that only he knew how to make money in the wine business out here and proceeded to base much of his wine on imported grapes. The finger wagging by the competition on that point was somewhat hypocritical in that several other Long Island wineries were using off-island grapes, some more openly than others.

In the 80s some very fine merlots and chardonnays were made from grapes from the winery's North Fork vineyards by Le Rêve's first winemaker, Robert Bethel. Nonetheless, a groan could be heard on the East End when Alan Barr appeared on the cover of the *Wine Spectator* in November, 1988. The community was delighted by the recognition by the bible of wine lovers, and by the statement on the cover that "Long Island has arrived." But if only the photo on the cover didn't show Barr, jaunty and confident in his white suit and red bow tie, holding a glass of chardonnay and standing on an acre of perfect lawn that stretched back to his red brick, Norman winery.

The prevailing reaction wasn't one of sorrow when, not long after the

Russell Hearn

opening of the winery, rumors of overextension and financial difficulty started to circulate. When Russell Hearn, a talented and experienced winemaker from Australia arrived at Le Rêve in 1990, Barclay's Bank was in the process of foreclosing on the mortgage. When they eventually succeeded they renamed the enterprise Southampton Winery and it was under that label, and under trying conditions, that Russell managed to make some respectable wines from the 1991 vintage. Alan Barr disappeared from the scene to which he never seemed to belong and Russell Hearn moved on to the newly established, and more tranquil Pellegrini Vineyards. Pindar's Herodotus Damianos, recognizing the potential in the Le Rêve location, its facility, and its equipment and recognizing a bargain, purchased the winery for around $2 million and created Duck Walk.

The community's feelings about the demise of the Mattituck Hills winery was quite different. John Simicich, a builder by profession, and his wife Cathy were straightforward, honest folk who fit well into the farming and grape-growing community of the North Fork. As with many of their peers, the Simicichs stretched themselves financially and emotionally to pursue their calling. They planted their first grape vines in 1983. When they decided to add winemaking to their grape growing operation, they sold virtually all their assets, including annuities and pensions, and negotiated a significant loan through Suffolk County to come up with the three quarters of a million dollars that they needed to build and equip the winery.

Although John was a self-taught winemaker, he managed to produce cabernets, merlots and chardonnays of some quality under his Mattituck Hills label. But John seemed blinded by his enthusiasm for his wines. His eagerness to acquire expensive barrels and equipment for his vineyards and cellar were neither controlled by financial judgement nor guided by a business plan. More loans were taken out, even on his children's houses, and as the winery slipped into the financial abyss, the family broke apart. The vineyards and winery now constitute a part of Macari Vineyards.

AN EXPANDING COMMUNITY

The crucial secret of the atomic bomb near the end of the Second World War was not any great formula, but rather the simple fact that the bomb was possible, that the laws of nature allowed a self-propagating nuclear reaction. Similarly, the modest explosion of wines that started to emerge from the Hargrave cellars in 1976, even with their variable quality, constituted proof that it could be done. Quality table wine could be produced on eastern Long Island from both red and white vinifera grapes.

Word started to get around, first locally, then around New York City, aided by articles in the *New York Times* and the *New Yorker*. By 1980, three others, Lyle Greenfield at Bridgehampton, Herodotus Damianos at Pindar, and Peter and Patricia Lenz, had followed the Hargrave's path.

It's a pattern familiar in new wine regions around the world: first come the vineyards and wineries; then supporting service industries; and then the businesses that accommodate visitors drawn to the region. Gradually, a community is born. The character of a small new wine region is determined by the personalities and world views of a handful of individuals. For the most part, the builders of the Long Island wine region, the entrepreneurs and winemakers who followed in the Hargrave's footsteps, are still working on the East End.

David Mudd

The primary importance of vineyard management has been an increasingly prominent theme of the Long Island wine industry. One speaks of "wine growing" and the statement that "the wine is made in the vineyard" has become almost a cliché. It is fitting, therefore, that the second person to play a prominent role in the development of the region after the Hargraves was David Mudd, who never made wine but who planted more than half of the original vineyards on the East End.

In 1974 Dave had recently retired as an airline pilot and had decided to grow turf on Long Island. He heard about the Hargraves from his son's father-in-

law who had installed the electrical wiring at the new winery and decided to find out what was happening out there. As he talked with Alex he became intrigued by the possibility of growing grapes. When Alex offered to sell him an acre's worth of the grapes he had ordered the die was cast. The next year David went to California to procure his own vines and, with his son, Steve, planted them on 15 additional acres. By 1978 they had 27 acres under vine and were selling grapes to home winemakers. This, according to Dave, had its own perils: "They would come out and buy a hundred pounds, or two hundred pounds. The only problem was that they would bring you a bottle of last year's wine, and after about four tastes of this high alcohol stuff you'd fall flat on your ass!"

The big-framed, affable, salty, but no-nonsense Dave Mudd became a ubiquitous and influential presence in Long Island wine country. In 1981 he became the first president of the Long Island Grape Growers Association,

David Mudd

which was later transformed into the L. I. Wine Council. In those days prospective winery owners would read about the Hargraves in the paper and travel out to Cutchogue. Alex would always try to discourage them. "Don't get into this business," Alex would say, "you'll lose your shirt." and if they insisted Alex would send them down to Dave. Dave had a different attitude: "People would come to us and want to lose a lot of money in the grape and wine business, and we'd help them."

Dave planted vineyards for Palmer, Pindar and what is now Pellegrini. In addition to consulting, planting and managing vineyards and growing grapes on his own thirty-seven acres, Dave has provided a host of ancillary services to a growing community of grape growers. With a graft cutter purchased early on he did thousands of graftings in the early years. Entrepreneurial and innovative, he avidly sought out new vineyard technology. He learned about underground trickle irrigation from the Israelis and became an early advocate, installing the first system at Island Vineyards (now Pellegrini) in 1982. He introduced a mechanical vine lifter to raise up the trellis wires during the growing season and a leaf plucker and hedger from New Zealand. In the 1990s Dave's ambition exceeded his business sense and some major initiatives, such as a wine storage and distribution service, turned out to be costly mistakes.

In recent years, Dave has turned over active management of the Mudd Vineyard and their consulting and vineyard management business to Steve. After twenty-five years in the business, Steve, handsome and articulate, is almost as savvy as his father, and is the most experienced of the second generation viniculturists on Long Island. His meticulous management of the family vineyard, and others that he manages such as Raphael, continues to set a high standard for the region.

Dan Kleck

Dan Kleck

While many of the winery owners tend to be independent and competitive, the winemakers of Long Island are often more communicative among themselves and more mobile, providing a beneficial cross-fertilization of ideas and experience. Dan Kleck was a good example. His winemaking career wound through the region in the early days like a connecting thread, contributing strength and color to the fabric of the community.

Dan had the clean cut, athletic look of a high school football star, along with the easy confidence that is often the long term reward of early athletic prowess. He was drawn to Long Island in 1979 after a stint with the Tabor Hills Vineyard in Michigan. Impressed by the wines being produced by the Hargraves, particularly Alex's 100% malolactic-fermented chardonnay, he applied to them for a job and was hired on as cellar rat. From the Hargraves, he absorbed the Long Island-French concept, and over time he earned the title of assistant winemaker.

By 1983, Dan felt that if he was to continue to learn and develop as a winemaker, he had to leave the fold of his mentors. He first worked as a manager of an ambitious winery project involving Island Vineyards, which eventually collapsed for financial reasons. He then consulted for many of the region's new enterprises, including Bridgehampton, managed vineyards and made wine for Peconic Bay, Lenz and Jamesport. During this time Dan was also one of the central organizers of the two influential symposia that brought winemakers from Bordeaux to Long Island. He gradually spent more and more time with Bidwell Vineyards and, in 1989, when the Bidwells gave him the scope he was seeking to create his own style of wines, he signed on full time. At the end of 1990, in a disagreement over salary, Dan left Bidwell and took a job with a new winery in Chile. Soon, however, he was lured back to Long Island by Bob Palmer and, in the summer of 1991, Dan became winemaker and manager at Palmer Vineyards.

Dan's predecessor as winemaker at Palmer was Gary Patzwald whose style of winemaking emphasized clean, crisp, fruit-driven wines, quite different from the darker, more complex wines, more influenced by oak and often hinting at dried fruits and wood, favored by Dan. Soon, the Kleck style prevailed at Palmer. For better or worse, this story is typical of a new wine region. When an estate is young and lacks a well established style, a change of winemaker can have a significant impact on the winery's product. This also means that someone like Dan Kleck, with his skill as a winemaker, his breadth of experience, his confidence and his communicative personality, can have a significant impact on the whole region's approach to winemaking. Influences are difficult to pin down, but several of Dan Kleck's enthusiasms, for instance for cabernet franc and sauvignon blanc, the latter made in a Bordeaux style, for late harvest riesling, and the active aeration of his red wines, are now widely shared on Long Island.

When Jess Jackson, of Kendall-Jackson fame, visited Long Island in 1998 speculation around the vineyards had it that a major investment in the region was imminent. Instead, Jackson hired Dan Kleck to be in charge of white wines at his new Monterey facility. Dan couldn't resist the challenge, part of which was simply one of scale. At Palmer, he worked with 400 barrels; in California he's working with 40,000. When Dan moved, the region lost one of its most capable and influential winemakers, but this move also represented an endorsement of the region. Some see Dan as Long Island's first settler on "the other coast."

THE LEARNING PROCESS

Part of the explanation of the rapidity of Long Island's qualitative growth as a wine region resides in the community's active process of research and learning. This has included everything from regular wine-tasting dinners of the wine-makers to a series of community symposia to the research and lecture programs of the Cornell Cooperative Extension Service.

The Symposia

In the summer of 1988, the first of a series of international wine symposia was produced by the Long Island winemakers. The Bordeaux Symposium, as it has come to be known, stressed strong similarities of climate between the East End of Long Island and the Bordeaux region. The symposium was held only fifteen years after the first vinifera wine grapes were planted on Long Island, no longer than a heartbeat on traditional viticultural time scales. Even so, some of Bordeaux's most knowledgeable viticulturists and most eminent winemakers attended. Paul Pontallier, the General Manager of Château Margaux was there, as was Mme. de Lencquesaing, the owner of Château Pichon-Longueville Comtesse de Lalande (usually referred to as Château Lalande) and Alain Carbonneau of the French National Institute of Agronomic Research. The United States was also represented by winemakers from Connecticut, Pennsylvania, Rhode Island and Virginia as well as California. Attending the symposium one was reminded of the old saying that water separates the people of the world; wine unites them.

Paul Pontallier

The technical topics discussed included the initiation of malolactic fermentation; chemical evolution of oak used in barrels, and its effects on flavors in wine; chemical properties of soils; and vine canopy management. Equally important were the many formal and informal occasions to sample Long Island wines, some of which use the same grapes prominent in Bordeaux: cabernet sauvignon, cabernet franc and merlot.

As they visited the wineries and participated in comparative tastings, the visitors were impressed. Some of Long Island's sauvignon blancs were judged

61

"better than anything in the Loire Valley." Château Margaux's Pontallier was quoted as saying, "I like Long Island's Merlot better than California's because the bouquet is truer to form." Surprisingly, Monsieur Pontallier also revealed a bit of envy for his Long Island confreres. In the principal wine areas of France strict laws (Appellation d'Origine Controllée) control virtually every aspect of winemaking: not only the particular plots of land and varieties of grapes that can be bottled under a specific label, but also how the vines must be fertilized and pruned, and the number of grapes that can be harvested per hectare. Pontallier said, "You know that we carry on a very old tradition with many important ancestors, and sometimes I have the desire to make vineyards, to plant vines in new areas like you are doing." Eleven years later, Pontallier would confirm his interest in Long Island by participating in Raphael, a new winery on the North Fork.

The Bordeaux Symposium gave a shot-in-the-arm to Long Island winemaking. It added to the growing publicity given to the region and communicated technical advice to the practitioners. The French visitors surprised their hosts by spending more time in the vineyards than in the cellars. Gerald Asher quotes Richard Olsen-Harbich, as saying, "They really made quite an impression…More than anything else, the visit helped us change our focus. Until the French came we had been so preoccupied with winemaking that we hadn't fully grasped the importance of what we were doing in the vineyard."

The Bordeaux Symposium also bolstered the Long Islanders' collective confidence that they could make the big time, and it augmented their sense of community and coherence as a group of winemakers who were in the process of defining a significant new wine region. Fittingly enough, in that July of 1988, while the French visitors and their hosts and hostesses were listening to lectures, tramping through vineyards and generally comparing notes, the nearby grapes were quietly ripening into what would later be called "the vintage to put Long Island on the map."

Two years later, as those 1988 wines were beginning to appear from the winemakers' cellars, the group hosted another symposium, this time focussed on the emerging red wine grape for Long Island, merlot. The 1990 Merlot Symposium attracted a plethora of industry leaders. From Pomerol, the Bordeaux region which has the world's most famous merlot vineyards, came Michel Rolland, owner and enologist at the renowned Château Le Bon Pasteur. Some of the most prominent West Coast makers of Merlot wines were there: Duckhorn Vineyards from Napa Valley, Clos du Bois Winery from Sonoma County, and Columbia Winery and The Hogue Cellars, both from Washington State.

The Historical Legacy

On the first day of the symposium Alain Querre, owner of Château Monbousquet in St. Emilion, cautioned the upstart winemakers of the New World that "it takes two or three generations to create a new vineyard of quality in a vine growing area where they have never produced a wine of quality in the past," and added that, judging from the history of the French regions and châteaux, "it takes more than a century to build the reputation of a vine-growing area such as Pomerol or St. Emilion." Nonetheless, at the end of the week, M. Querre carried merlots from Bidwell and Bedell Cellars back to France with him saying, "They're better than anything made in California."

Other symposia would follow over the years, for example, one on chardonnay and one on managing the tannins in wine. All would be useful but, as the region matured, none would have the impact of the Bordeaux Symposium of 1988.

Cornell Cooperative Extension

In the beginning – that is in 1973 - wine growing on Long Island was a pure experiment. The Hargraves and their followers had to determine empirically what grape varieties would work, how they should be managed in the vineyard, how to fend off pests and diseases, and what vinification techniques were most effective. In carrying out that critical process the vineyard managers and wine-makers have had an important ally in the Cornell Cooperative Extension of Suffolk County, and particularly in its viticulturist, Alice Wise.

Driving along Sound Avenue in the town of Riverhead, it is easy to be distracted by the scenic farmland and not notice the unassuming building that houses the Cooperative Extension. A public service offshoot of Cornell University, the Extension provides advice on crop cultivation and management throughout the state. The part of this service that deals with viticulture is largely centered at the New York Experimental Station in Geneva, which is a recognized source on vineyard management practices.

The viticulture program on Sound Avenue is decidedly more modest, currently consisting of Alice Wise. But, because of Alice's dedication and energy, her program's impact on the community has been out of proportion to its size. She is a consultant to the wineries, runs educational programs and workshops, issues newsletters, and conducts research on topics of particular concern to the industry. With a degree in Horticulture from the University of Maryland, Alice did graduate work in the Pomology Department at Cornell where she earned her degree with a thesis on pest management. Concerning her current interest in viticulture, Alice explains "I was bitten by a bug (and became) consumed with interest about vineyards and winemaking."

When Alice took on the position of viticultural education specialist at the beginning of 1987, one of her unexpected tasks was to overcome the skepticism of Long Island growers who felt that they had been misled by the upstate specialists into adopting viticultural practices unsuitable to the Island. The Cornell experts offered what they then understood based on viticultural experience from upstate, where climate and soil are vastly different from the North Fork. In particular, their knowledge was largely limited to hybrids of native varietals, whose requirements vary considerably from those of European vinifera that form the basis of Long Island viticulture.

Recent years have seen a broadening of understanding based on the success of the Long Island experiments and Alice was a persuasive voice during this period of transition. As an indication of the changes in outlook since the first years, it is now possible for Alice to usefully adapt some of the ongoing research at the Agricultural Experimental Station in upstate Geneva, such as work on plant pathology, to the purposes of the Island.

One line of inquiry at the Long Island facility today concerns a systematic evaluation of grape clones. There are, for example, more than a dozen chardonnay clones that differ in flavor, as well as in cluster size, ripening times, and the ability to resist certain diseases. In earlier years, grapes were planted on Long Island using whatever clonal types were commercially available, without much thought being given to their suitability. However, as Alice remarks, different clones planted on the same site make different wines. The varietals themselves perform in significantly different ways depending on terrain and climate. Alice cultivates two acres of vines in which the choices of grapes and clones are varied. She vinifies these in small lots, using no wood in the fermentation process, to produce wines that accentuate the character of the grapes, and of different clones of the same grapes. The results are then reported to the winemaking community in a series of seminars and tastings that reveal the effect of changing the nutrient levels, the amount of crop thinning, and the impact of early versus late harvesting. The results are of significance in terms of identifying new grapes to plant and of clones of those grapes that would produce wines of greater character than from those used more or less haphazardly planted in the past.

Another prominent line of inquiry for Alice is the issue of pest management and the control of plant diseases, especially the use of pesticides. She looks at how predators can be introduced to reduce certain pests in place of chemicals, for example. Since the contamination of ground water supplies by pesticides is of grave concern on Long Island, this line of investigation is being followed closely by environmentalists as well as vineyard managers.

The decision to give priority to one research issue over another is reached in consultation with an Advisory Committee consisting of four local growers and winemakers who help Alice set her agenda. Her greatest contribution, she feels, is facilitating the flow of information to the industry by publishing frequent newsletters about her findings, arranging seminars on topics of relevance, and inviting wine experts from elsewhere to give talks of local interest. She understands that her work must complement the experiments carried out by the wineries, helping them to learn "how to read a vineyard." It is clear that the experimental phase of the development of the Long Island wine region is far from over and that the Extension Service will have a continuing, important role.

THE SELLING OF THE WINES

The successful development of a new wine region requires show as well as substance. It is not enough to make fine wines; the wine buying public must be aware that such wines are being produced and must be willing to buy them. Although it may not have the same romantic appeal as growing grapes or fermenting wine in French oak barrels, marketing is no less important, and no less time consuming. To many fledgling winemakers on Long Island, it has seemed to be the hardest part of all. The most obvious advantage of the region, its proximity to one of the largest and most sophisticated wine markets in the world, at times has seemed a disadvantage because of the infinite number of wines that are already available to the New York market. But that market beckons irresistibly to the Long Island producer, not only because of its size, but also because it can be served at low cost directly from the wineries, avoiding the twenty-five or thirty percent normally charged by distributors.

Long Island wines made inroads into the New York restaurant and wine store market (and from there to other parts of the world) first by the individual efforts of the savvy Alex Hargrave, and then through the knowledgeable efforts of Lyle Greenfield of Bridgehampton Winery and Bob Palmer of Palmer Vineyards, both of whom worked in the advertising field. By the mid-1980s, the region was starting to receive serious attention by the wine world.

National attention came with the publication of the "Long Island Has Arrived" cover article in the *Wine Spectator* of November, 1989. Eighty different wines from nine Long Island wineries were rated in the article; thirteen of those were awarded scores of at least eighty-eight on the *Spectator's* one hundred point scale. In the same issue a number of French wines, such as a Château Haut-Batailley, an Echézeaux and a Châteauneuf-du-Pape, scored in the low eighties. That issue reflected the interest of the *Spectator's* influential editor, Marvin Shanken, in Long Island wines and marked the beginning of the *Spectator's* regular coverage of the area.

The Wine Spectator appeals to serious wine mavens. Its recognition does not necessarily mean public acceptance. A more telling indication of the growth of the popularity of Long Island wines was a series of remarkable wine tasting parties held on Long Island and in New York. These affairs turned out to be highly effective promotional events and, also took the popular pulse of the industry. At each occasion the industry was found to be healthier than even the winery owners realized.

In the spring of 1990 word spread about a benefit barbecue and barrel tasting of Long Island wines being organized by the Long Island Wine Council and *The Wine Spectator*. The party would benefit Lyme Disease research at the University Hospital at Stony Brook. The driving forces behind the affair were Alex and Louisa Hargrave and Marvin Shanken, the editor and publisher of the *Spectator*. Alex had suffered seriously from an undiagnosed case of Lyme disease, and his vineyard would be the site of the party.

The theme of the party was the celebration not only of Long Island wines but also the rich produce of the Island. Many of the Island's best chefs were there along with the winery owners and winemakers. The synergy between Long Island's produce, cuisine and wines would continue to run through the promotion of Long Island wines in the future. The wineries used the occasion of the first barrel tasting party to release their still unbottled 1989 merlots, which the attendees tasted from glasses filled from the barrel.

The organizers originally wondered whether enough people would be persuaded to pay $100 each to taste Long Island wines and local fare, albeit for a good cause. They had expected about 500 people to sign up for the barrel tasting. Acceptances soon passed that point and they added another tent. Eventually, when they reached the limit of 900, they had to mail back over 100 checks.

Party day was clear and cloudless, with just enough breeze to temper the August sun. The Porsches, Jaguars and immaculately restored wooden station wagons that arrived in the Hargraves' field parking lot indicated that the Hamptons set had decided that this was the place to be. Under the first tent the lively crowd, generally clad in studiously informal chic, happily downed Long Island chardonnays, rieslings, cabernets, merlots and sparkling wines, accompanied by hors d'oeuvres made from local seafood, game and vegetables. Later they moved to long tables covered with red checked table cloths. Before the evening was over, and the bluegrass and zydeco bands played their last notes, an entire 280-pound swordfish had been devoured, along with 800 lobsters, 900 ears of local corn, 900 breasts of ducks from the South Fork, and eleven bushels of peaches from just down the road.

Did the popular appeal of Long Island wines extend beyond the Island? The question was tested with another combined tasting with Long Island food, this time at a New York City wine and food mecca, Windows on the World, on May 7, 1991. This was the time of the greatest effectiveness of the Long Island Wine Council, very much due to its executive director, Phil Nugent. Once again the response exceeded the Wine Council's expectations, and the event had to be limited to the first 1000 aspirants. Word had clearly gotten around and the palpable excitement of the evening made clear that Long Island wines were no longer a bright secret of Long Islanders. The cat was out of the bag.

The following years saw a series of similar events, each better attended – and more expensive - than its predecessor. The barrel tastings continued until 1996 when organizational fatigue, increasingly strict health department regulations, and escalating costs got the better of them. Meanwhile tourist visits to the vineyards continued to increase and the individual wineries created their own events: tastings, picnics, concerts, hayrides, to attract visitors. The New York "Windows on Long Island" remains a staple.

In the wine region's early stages and then in the 90's its public relations was facilitated by a generally sympathetic press. An irrepressible upstart joined the Long Island wine scene in 1992 in the form of the *Wine Press*, soon transformed into the *GrapeZine*. The creation of Michael Todd, the *'Zine* chronicled the wine scene on Long Island with care and affection in a gossipy irreverent style until Todd's death in 1998. Over the years *The Wine Spectator* showed a continuing interest in Long Island. Periodically, Thomas Matthews, its executive editor, would write a knowledgeable article identifying regional high points and gauging the region's progress. Alan J. Wax at *Newsday* became a sympathetic observer of the Long Island wine scene and in 1999 the *New York Times* published a notable series of well researched and insightful articles by Howard G. Goldberg.

The blind tasting: It's a risky strategy, but it has worked for Long Island. In 1988, for example, Larry Perrine took six Long Island 1996 chardonnays to California for a head-to-head blind tasting with some of Sonoma County's leading bottlings. The results sounded more like a dream of the LI Wine Council than the product of a strict comparative tasting run by the Sonoma County Winemakers Technical Group; the wines of Bedell, Palmer and Peconic Bay took first, second, and third place ahead of Acacia, Morgan and Wild Horse.

Long Island wine makers have even dared to put their wines up against the best that France can offer in blind tastings. Lenz Winery has been the most enterprising in arranging these shoot-outs that have been held in San Francisco, Paris and New York, as well as on the Island. Lenz's wines have scored right up there with the likes of La Grande Dame champagne, Chateau Pétrus and Drouin's Montrachet Marquis de Laguiche. There are good bases for questioning the scoring process in such tastings, particularly when the judges know there are great wines in the set. Nonetheless, there is no doubt about the publicity value in the results.

Any winemaker takes delight in fooling the experts in blind tastings. For Long Island a particularly satisfying example occurred in 1991 in the course of an annual four-day wine extravaganza in New York called the New York Wine Experience. In one of the seminar/tastings wine professionals were asked to identify various wines. One of the tasters was Jancis Robinson, a highly respected wine authority and writer. *The New York Times* reported that, after tasting an unidentified chardonnay, she said, "I thought it was a Chassagne Montrachet," referring to one of the great white wines of Burgundy. "And I was sitting next to a British wine merchant with a very good palate. He thought the same thing." The wine turned out to be a 1989 Chardonnay from Gristina.

THE EFFECTS OF LEGISLATION

Potential winery owners as well as local farmers and grape growers act within a framework of price structures and laws. The history of the Long Island wine region has been strongly affected in various ways by legislation at the federal, state and local level. New York Governor Hugh Cary was a staunch supporter of the state's wine industry and encouraged the legislature to pass the 1976 Farm Winery Bill that provided tax incentives to small-scale wineries. Subsequent bills allowed the wineries to hold tastings and to sell wine on Sundays. As it has turned out, sales from their tasting rooms have been crucial for the financial viability of many Long Island wineries.

Suffolk County's Farmland Preservation Legislation has also played a crucial role in making vineyards a financially feasible option. Although the East End of Long Island has traditionally been a farming area, the value of land has increasingly been set by its value for houses and shopping centers. Farmers have seen their taxes continually increase in response to that value. They have also come to realize that they could sell their farms, put the money in the bank, and receive a higher income for sitting in the Florida sun than for their current hard labors. That more farmers have not yielded to that temptation is eloquent testimony to their devotion to a family tradition and way of life that, in many cases, is many generations old.

The Historical Legacy

Soon after taking office as County Executive in 1972, John V. N. Klein identified the "perpetuation of farming and the consequent preservation of open space" as a priority of his administration. The vehicle that emerged to accomplish that objective was a program whereby the County would buy the development rights of farms and other open spaces. That is, the farmer would sell the right to convert the land to other than farming use for an amount equal to the difference between its value as a farm and its value on the open market. Klein was having trouble convincing the legislature of the wisdom of his proposal until he took a group of leaders out to see John Wickham. As Klein described it recently, "He piled his apples around them; he talked about his family, and when he was through, the entire proposition was sold." The enabling legislation was passed in 1974 and the first rights were acquired by the county in 1977.

That legislation has slowed the rate of conversion of farmland into shopping malls and housing developments. In a benefit never anticipated by its writers, it has also promoted an entirely new form of high value agriculture: the growing of wine grapes. In the 1980s and 90s the price of land on the East End fluctuated with economic cycles. Between early 1998 and the end of 1999 the price of farmland on the North Fork with development rights intact rose by 10–20% because of a flurry of interest in planting vineyards. By the end of the millenium, an acre of farmland with development rights intact fetched $20,000 - $25,000, and in some cases as much as $30,000. At that price, growing grapes for sale to winemakers (at around $1,500 per ton) was uneconomical. A better case could be made for growing grapes and making wine yourself, but even in that case the sheer cost of holding land would amount to around $1.00 a bottle. However, if the development rights were sold off (at $8,000 – $10,000), the land would cost about half as much ($12,000-$15,000 an acre) which makes a significant difference in the profitability of the venture.

The tax laws of the 1970s and early 80s were favorable to investment in farms and vineyards. By 1985, the region's land under vines had grown to about 1400 acres. The 1985 tax laws, however, reduced a number of favorable tax writeoffs. In particular, the new laws required an absentee owner to be an active participant in the vineyard operations in order to take a tax loss. This contributed to the minimal growth in the region between 1985 and 1998. As the millenium neared its end, however, the reputation of the region burgeoned and a new wave of investments began to be made, without federal tax inducement. At the end of 1999 there were about 2000 acres under vines and, given current plans, that number will soon reach 2500 acres.

Chapter IV
Vineyards and Wineries

Wine is...constant proof that God loves us and loves to see us happy.
—Benjamin Franklin

*I*n this chapter we provide brief descriptions of each winery and attempt to capture elements of their style and individuality. There is no attempt to rate specific wines since vintages disappear from the market all too quickly. Moreover, rankings are always subjective and vary according to vintage. For up-to date listings of the wines available at each winery, with prices, and a list of retailers on Long Island and New York City who feature these wines, consult the quarterly publication called *The Wine Press* (PO Box 1500, Mattituck, NY).

We profile twenty-five wineries in alphabetical order. Their locations are indicated on the map provided at the end of the book. Following each profile is an address, phone number and, if available, a web-site, together with a list of the principals. An industry-wide web-site can be found at www.longislandwinecountry.com.

We strongly suggest that you visit the web-sites or call for information about special events that take place at the wineries, the hours in which the tasting rooms are open, and for a list of the wines available for sale. Everyone accepts most credit cards and are handicap-accessible. Except in a few cases, each winery provides complimentary tastings during visiting hours and a few offer special tours of the facilities. Call ahead for details or, better yet, take a ride out on some lovely day in the late spring or early autumn (summer crowds can make tastings a bit hectic, especially on weekends) and drop in for a visit. You will find friendly and welcoming people who are eager to have you try their wines. If a particular wine appeals to you, pick up a couple of bottles. Usually there are substantial discounts for purchases by the case. A few wineries, such as Pugliese, even have picnic areas under shaded arbors.

As this book goes to press some wineries are undergoing a period of transition as new owners take the helm. The current winemaking teams may also change, and even the very name of the winery and labels they use may be altered. After some consideration we regrettably decided to relegate one of these transitional properties to a section at the end of this chapter that is entitled "The Changing Wine Scene." We also include there those nascent operations that are expected to come on-line in the new millennium with a selection of wines and a tasting room for the public.

The porch at Pindar

Bedell Cellars

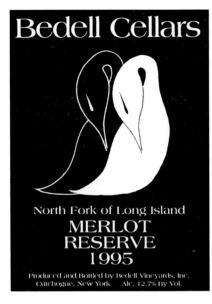

Bedell Cellars

North Fork of Long Island
**MERLOT
RESERVE
1995**

Produced and Bottled by Bedell Vineyards, Inc.
Cutchogue, New York   Alc. 12.7% By Vol.

The worn gravel driveway that leads to the Bedell Cellars winery in Cutchogue skirts a traditional Long Island farmhouse, shaded by maples and close on to Route 25. The sign out front carries the Bedell black and white swan logo, but the farm looks much like the numerous potato-growing homesteads that dot the landscape of Eastern Long Island. It conjures up images of fresh vegetables and road-side stands, not of refined wines.

Across the driveway from the house is a sign with a painted silhouette, warning the driver that the farmyard cats may be at play in the road ahead. The winery building is a barn reconstructed in a practical, businesslike manner. The one concession to the upscale is a pair of stained glass panels in the doors to the tasting room. A worn pick-up truck is sometimes parked outside, completing the overall impression of a small-scale farming operation that has changed little over the generations.

Behind the small tasting room is a winery's equivalent of the farm kitchen: a combination office and laboratory with a jumble of technical books and journals, coffee cups, bottles (mostly open), test tubes and meters of various kinds, a small desk, a few miscellaneous chairs, file cabinets, a small computer, and a black Labrador curled up on the floor.

Kip Bedell started to make wine as a hobby in the basement of his West Hempstead home more than twenty-five years ago. First using concentrated grape juice, and then grapes from up-state New York, he would produce one to two hundred gallons a year, and year-by-year, he would learn from the traditional teacher of winemaking: trial and error. An early lesson was that wine can only be as good as the grapes that go into it.

As he became more ambitious for his wines and increasingly more consumed by his hobby, Kip found it harder and harder to procure grapes of high enough quality. He started to muse over the possibility of a vineyard of his own. Familiar with the North Fork from childhood memories of summers spent with grandparents in Mattituck, Kip was naturally drawn to the then infant vineyard country on Long Island. He and his wife Susan bought fifty acres of land in Cutchogue that had been known as the Davids Farm in the previous 200 years and planted his first seven acres of vines in 1980. Kip continued to plant over the next three years until nineteen acres that were once potato fields were covered with vinifera grape vines.

Kip is a quiet, thoughtful man whose apparently easy-going and laid-back manner belies a dedication and passion for the business of making fine wine. He describes himself as a self-taught vintner with only a modest bolstering by some courses in wine related chemistry in Pennsylvania. He continues to apply a persistent, intelligent trial and error approach to more and more sophisticated challenges of wine making.

Bedell's first vintage, in 1985, was nearly derailed by Hurricane Gloria that headed straight for the East End of Long Island packing winds that would tear many of the grapes from their vines. Kip admits it was the worst experience of his winemaking years and, quite naturally, he would just as soon consider 1986 to be his first real vintage. In that first year Kip was advised by Gary Patzwald, who had become the winemaker at Palmer Vineyards.

Kip seems equally comfortable in jeans and workboots atop a tractor in the vineyard, in the winery laboratory, or buttoned down in suit and tie pouring samples and talking about his wine in the tasting room. One suspects, however, that he is happiest outside on that tractor, or in the wine room making wine. In the vineyard, Kip depends strongly on his vineyard manager, Dave Thompson, who previously worked at the nearby Ressler Vineyards.

Bedell Cellars produces two styles of chardonnay, one of which is fermented in stainless steel and the other is barrel fermented. Both exhibit understated power and elegance, with the barrel fermented bottling being somewhat creamier and richer. There is also an attractive gewürztraminer, a riesling ice wine that exudes intriguing pineapple scents, and a viognier. It is safe to say, however, that the star at Bedell is merlot which one renowned wine commentator has dubbed the "benchmark merlot" of Long Island. About half of Bedell's production is devoted to this varietal which exhibits, especially in the Reserve, dark berry fruit, a peppery spiciness, and a creamy texture. These wines are aged mostly in American oak barrels, which imparts an agreeable layer of toastiness to the wine. Kip has experimented with oak from Minnesota, Missouri and Kentucky and is still trying out new coopers.

Though some Long Island winemakers eschew cabernet sauvignon in favor of merlot because the latter requires a shorter growing season and is more predictable, Kip Bedell, remains steadfastly committed to his cabernet wines. He says that the secret is curbing the vine's prolific growth habits by proper leaf canopy pruning and by proper site selection. The Cabernet Reserve is, like the

73

Reserve Merlot, a rich, intense, but supple wine that conveys mineral and smoky tobacco scents imparted by the charred American oak barrels. Kip is careful to apply some restraint in the use of these barrels since their aggressiveness, compared to the milder flavors imparted by French oak barrels, can bestow a pungent aroma reminiscent of a freshly opened box of crayola, something he manages to avoid.

There is also a blend of cabernet sauvignon and merlot, with some cabernet franc added in, called Cupola. Though Cupola may not be quite as deep or as complex as the Reserve bottlings of merlot or cabernet sauvignon, it remains a fine wine. Bedell also sells a zippy but straightforward quaffing wine, known as Main Road Red.

For the consumer, one of the problems with Bedell Cellar's premium wines is that demand exceeds supply. While Kip Bedell says this is the kind of problem he likes to have, it does mean that some of the wines tend to be released sooner than they should be. Particularly for the reds, we suggest that a few years in the cellar will reward the buyer.

Beginning in 2000, Kip's venerable winery has a new owner, Michael Lynne, President of New Line Cinemas and also the current owner of Corey Creek Vineyards. However, Kip will remain as winemaker for the next several years. Bedell's current annual production is some 8,000 cases, a figure which will continue to rise as Bedell Cellars gradually expands on the thirty two acres now under cultivation.

When Kip wore two hats, as owner in addition to general manager and winemaker, he was able to mediate between the needs of winemaker and the fiscal realities of proprietor in favor of maintaining quality. He is now be able to focus his talents completely on the winemaking and there is every expectation that the wines reaching the consumer will be as good, if not better, than ever.

Bedell Cellars

Address: Route 25, Cutchogue
Owners: Kip and Susan Bedell
Winemaker: Kip Bedell
Vineyard Manager: Dave Thompson
Phone: (631) 734-7537
Web-site: www.bedellcellars.com

Bidwell Vineyards

Estate Bottled
1995

BIDWELL

SAUVIGNON BLANC

NORTH FORK OF LONG ISLAND

ALCOHOL 12.5% BY VOLUME

Bidwell Vineyards is one of the oldest family-owned and operated wineries on Long Island. It was established by Robert Bidwell and his wife Patricia, in 1982, with a first release in 1986. Located on the North Fork's north road, the winery has generally been overshadowed by some of its more glamorous peers even though it has consistently provided well crafted quality wines at reasonable prices from its thirty or so acres of vineyards. It has always been a low key operation that sells most of the seven or eight thousand cases it produces annually from what for a long time was a rather modest tasting room. There was also a period of time when Bidwell's fortunes ebbed and there were even rumors of bankruptcy. Fortunately, with ownership now in the hands of Bidwell's three sons Bob, James, and Kerry, the tide has turned. A handsome and larger tasting room has replaced its less inviting predecessor and the wines are better than ever.

Bidwell Vineyards

For the first few years winemaking was in the hands of Dan Kleck, who later moved on to Palmer Vineyards, followed for a time by Mark Friszolowski, now winemaker at Pindar Vineyards. They established a style of wine in which the preservation of clear varietal characteristics was paramount. Since then Bob Bidwell has been in charge of vineyard and cellar operations, and he has maintained this early vision of winemaking. He aims to cull a harvest of healthy grapes and then, in his words ,"not mess it up, keeping it simple." Bob manipulates the wine as little as possible, with little or no filtering, "letting the fruit shine through," as he puts it.

Merlot and cabernet sauvignon are the primary red wine grapes, with chardonnay, riesling, and sauvignon blanc as the dominant whites. Sauvignon blanc is generally not as productive a vine as chardonnay, and is less well known by consumers. Bidwell's Sauvignon Blanc, however, has become a signature wine at this property, eclipsing in popularity its fine chardonnay. It emphasizes melon and pineapple aromas at the expense of the more customary herbal and grassy flavors of this varietal.

Older vintages of the savory merlot and cabernet sauvignon wines are sometimes re-released a half-decade later, and they provide the consumer with an unusual opportunity to taste some wonderful wines in their maturity from one of Long Island's enduring producers. Don't miss the chance.

Bidwell Vineyards

Address: Route 48, Cutchogue
Owners: Robert, James, and Kerry Bidwell
Winemaker: Robert Bidwell
Phone: (631) 734-5200

Castello di Borghese: Hargrave Vineyard

Even if it didn't produce fine wines, Hargrave Vineyard would be worth a visit for purely historic reasons. Founded in 1973 by Alex and Louisa Hargrave, this estate not only sparked an entirely new wine region, it also firmly established the winemaking style that the Long Island wine industry would follow for the first two decades of its existence. At the turn of the millennium, Hargrave Vineyard made a new kind of history.

True, the history of the East End isn't quite the same as that of Europe: Rome, for example. There you can visit the Borghese Gallery with its grand collections amassed in the 1600s by Cardinal Scipione Borghese, favorite nephew of Pope Paul V and Bernini's first patron. The collection includes Canova's marble portrait of Paolina Borghese, sister of Napoleon. And in Florence you can visit the grand neoclassical Palazzo Borghese, built by Paolina's husband, Prince Camillo Borghese in 1821.

But now Long Island has its own Borghese. In 1999, Marco Borghese (who, if he were a different kind of person, would justifiably call himself Prince Borghese), his American-born wife Ann Marie and a small group of investors bought Hargrave Vineyards. With this transaction, said to have been for close to $4 million, a member of one of Italy's historically most prominent families took responsibility for Long Island's historically most important winery.

Although he grew up on a large estate in Tuscany that produces, among other bounty, the family's wine and olive oil, Marco has no direct experience in the wine business. For some years he lived in Philadelphia and commuted to New York to manage a business importing luxury leather goods. When asked what brought him to become a winery owner, he responds in a magisterially-paced baritone, infused with the flavor of Italy, "the moon and the stars were in alignment." The alignment occurred at Thanksgiving time, 1998 when some friends brought Marco and Ann Marie to meet the Hargraves. Over the next months he came to realize "the great potential of Long Island as a wine region."

Marco Borghese has no intention to be an absentee landlord. He, Ann

77

Marie and their three children live in the house next to the barn that houses the production end of the winery. Nor is he one to abruptly overturn tradition. His expansion plans will respect the character of the property – including the old potato barns - and the value inherent in the Hargrave name and the reputation of their wines. Both Louisa and Alex Hargrave have been retained as consultants and their children, Anne and Alexander (Zander) work at the winery. "We will experiment with new ways of doing things," Marco says, "but the first focus will

*Hargrave
Vineyard*

be to keep the quality where it has been." Consistent with that aim, Marco has also retained the Hargrave winemaker and vineyard manager, Mark Terry.

One shouldn't expect a revolution from a Borghese, but there will be an evolution. The estate is now called Castello di Borghese: Hargrave Vineyard, and the operation will soon take on a Borghese character. Whatever that turns out to involve, it will entail style and the highest quality. Relaxed and casual as he may be, you get the impression that Marco Borghese will accept nothing less. Some changes are already clear. He feels, for example, that Hargrave wines deserve to be marketed more widely and more aggressively. Ann Marie is actively involved in that quest. Over the next two years, he also plans to double production, up to

78

as many as 20,000 cases per year, with the emphasis on the high-end wines.

Then there will be some more adventurous changes. Five or six acres of currently unproductive land will be planted to sangiovese, the traditional grape of Tuscany. Marco may also plant nebbiolo but understands that this grape is more problematic in this region. Recognizing the limited experience with such grapes among U.S. winemakers, Marco plans to use Italian winemaking consultants for the Italian varieties. Borghese family olive oil may also appear on the shelves at the winery. In the longer term, Marco would like to create something that responds to a widely recognized need in the region, a small hotel with a fine restaurant.

Visitors to the winery will still find the carefully crafted wines whose quality have for 25 years been guaranteed by the Hargrave name. At the top of the roster are the classical varietals bearing the lattice label: cabernet sauvignon, merlot, and chardonnay. Equally impressive are the Hargrave cabernet franc, pinot blanc and blanc fumé. Pinot noir is a famously tricky grape, but when the sun shines just right and Bacchus smiles, the Hargrave pinot can be one of the best on Long Island. All of these wines are made with a light hand, reflecting Alex Hargrave's aim that "the fruit ring true." It is finesse rather than power that has always characterized Hargrave wines. The winery also produces some notable inexpensive wines. One of the most popular quaffing wines on Long Island is their Chardonette, a clean, crisp, stainless steel-fermented chardonnay. The non-vintage Petit Châteaux red is also a bargain. In what is a laudable – and rare - practice, Castello di Borghese: Hargrave Vineyard also offers some of its older wines for sale at the winery.

This is still a personal and informal operation. When you call the winery the phone may well be answered by Anne Hargrave, or by a deep baritone voice that says "Hargrave Vineyard" with an aristocratic Italian accent.

Castello di Borghese: Hargrave Vineyard

Address: Route 48, Cutchogue
Owners: Marco and Ann Marie Borghese
Winemaker: Mark Terry
Vineyard Manager: Mark Terry
Phone: (631) 734-5111
Web-site: www.castellodiborghese.com

Channing Daughters

In what must be the most bucolic setting for a winery in all Long Island, Channing Daughters is serenely located among the farmlands that envelop Scuttlehole Road leading from Bridgehampton to Sag Harbor on the South Fork. The vineyards appear unannounced in the midst of adjacent cornfields. A gravel road leads to a small tasting room that once served as a farm shed. The neatly hedged vines are surrounded by whimsical wood sculptures dotting the veranda of the tasting room and even out among the vines. These sculptures from discarded tree stumps are prized works of art that are exhibited at prestigious galleries, such as the Elaine Benson Gallery in Bridgehampton. The artist is the winery owner Walter Channing, who is otherwise known as a successful venture capitalist and, with wife Molly, proprietor of about a hundred and twenty five acres of farmland and woods along Scuttlehole Road. Twenty five of these acres are currently being cultivated as vines, with another 35 or so in the process of being planted so that the current production of 4000 cases will shortly double. The winery opened to the public in 1998.

Larry Perrine, winemaker and, since 1996, Managing Partner with Walter Channing, has a long experience with the Long Island wine industry. Originally from California, where he trained in soil science and microbiology Larry came east to obtain a degree in enology and viticulture from Cornell University and then, starting in 1985, worked for David Mudd, the Island's most prominent vineyard developer and manager. This was followed by a stint at Cornell's grape research program on Long Island before joining the newly formed Gristina Vineyards in 1988. Larry was instrumental in catapulting Gristina into one of the Island's premier wineries but he left after several years to become a freelance consultant to a number of wineries in the Northeast. Eventually he hooked up with Walter Channing where he has since been pursuing a winemaking philosophy that contrasts strikingly with that of some other properties which put a premium on producing highly extracted wines that win awards at the expense of easy drinkability. Larry eschews this style of winemaking in favor of graceful wines that emphasize the primacy of fresh grape aromas, wines meant to enhance rather than overwhelm food. The key here is to craft wines that suit contemporary tastes in food, which lean increasingly towards lighter fare for which more ponderous oak-laden wines are ill matched. To achieve this goal Larry largely avoids malolactic fermentation and oak aging for white wines to preserve freshness, and is sparing in their use even for the reds. He wants to avoid the flavor of wood intruding on the fruit. "Less is more," he says.

The winery has been planting the white grape varietals pinot grigio, pinot bianco, and tocai friulano, as well as the red wine grape dolcetto, all from Northern Italy. These make wines that at their best are crisp, subtly aromatic, and freshly engaging, wines that encourage a drinker to take another sip. As some of these wines make their appearance in the Channing Daughters' portfolio over the next several years, there is currently available, among other wines, a delightfully herbal and mouthwatering sauvignon blanc from old vines planted by David Mudd, and a beaujolais-styled wine appropriately called "fresh red". Even the merlot and chardonnay, mainstay varietals at other Long Island wineries, are here given a deft touch in which a refreshing sappiness is clearly in evidence.

Larry Perrine and Walter Channing

Another reason for the unusual choice of grapes currently being planted is that Larry wants the fruit to ripen well. Terrain and climate conspire to limit the degree of maturity that some grapes can attain in a given region and he wants to avoid "being on the margin of the area". The secret to good wine, he says, is "ripe grapes," another of Larry's aphorisms that characterize his no-nonsense approach to wine.

The low key pastoral setting of the winery, Walter's uninhibited and breezy sculptures, and Larry's devotion to wines that are to be enjoyed without fuss form a winning combination that distinguishes this enterprise from all others on the Island.

Channing Daughters

Address: 1927 Scuttlehole Road, Bridgehampton
Owners: Walter and Molly Channing
Managing Partner and Winemaker: Larry Perrine
Vineyard Manager: John Witherspoon
Phone: (631) 537-7224
Web-site: www.channingdaughters.com

Corey Creek Vineyards

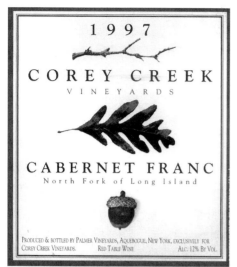

In a simple but attractive tasting room nestled among a patch of vines on Route 25 in Southold, Corey Creek Vineyards is a property in transition. As this book goes to press, the original owners, Joel and Peggy Lauber, have sold their holding to Michael Lynne, president of New Line Cinemas and a Long Island resident. The Lauber's will continue to manage Corey Creek until the beginning of the year 2001 and are responsible for all wine produced through the 1998 vintage.

The original 18 acres of vines that were planted in 1981 were acquired by the Laubers in 1993 after Joel sold his advertising business in New York City in order to pursue a new life style on Long Island. Today there are 30 acres in a bucolic setting that is bordered by two inlets from Peconic Bay, one of which is appropriately called Corey Creek. The annual production of some 4000 cases includes several acclaimed wines, especially the merlot and a reserve chardonnay. These are wines that "reflect the region," says Joel, and they are the embodiment of what the consumer has come to expect from a superior Long Island wine: soft textures combined with smoky berry aromas framed by a bit of oak nuances for the merlot, and crisp citrus, melon, and vanillin flavors for the chardonnay.

From the beginning the wines have been made by Dan Kleck and Russell Hearn, but Eric Fry of Lenz Vineyards will take on that responsibility under Mr. Lynne. Joel says that he saw his involvement with Corey Creek would be an interim activity to ease his transition into a life on the North Fork and so, when the opportunity arose to sell the property, he and Peggy did so. What happens now under the new ownership remains to be seen but there is every reason to believe that Corey Creek's repute will be maintained and, quite possibly, enhanced during the first decade of the millennium.

Corey Creek Vineyards
Address: Route 25, Southold
Owner: Michael Lynne
Winemaker : Eric Fry
Phone: (631) 765-4168
Web-site: www.liwines/coreycreek

Duck Walk Vineyards

DUCK WALK VINEYARDS
1996
RESERVE CHARDONNAY
LONG ISLAND, NEW YORK
PRODUCED AND BOTTLED BY DUCK WALK VINEYARDS
WATER MILL, SOUTHAMPTON, N.Y. ALC. 12.5% BY VOL.

Tangible evidence of the Long Island wine industry's maturity is that there at least one example of a second generation, parent to offspring, involvement, namely Duck Walk. Here, Jason Damianos, son of Dr. Herodotus Damianos, the proprietor of Pindar, is in charge of winemaking at the grandiose, Norman styled, copper roofed brick building in Water Mill. Together with his brother Alex, who is general manager, Jason has brought a new sense of commitment to the winery. Its reputation suffered in the past from the over-reaching ambitions of the original owner who had named the winery Le Rêve and following Le Rêve's bankruptcy, from its lackluster performance as Southampton Winery. When Damianos purchased the property in 1994 he had to revive its sagging fortunes by a massive investment in new vineyards, replacing the existing stock with 35 replanted acres, and by the purchase of an additional 35 acres that once belonged to the now defunct Mattituck Hills Winery on the North Fork. The most significant additions, however, are the recent changes in winemaking.

Jason, an intense and determined young man, spent many of his weekends and summers during high school on Long Island working among the vines at Pindar, under the tuteledge of the then winemaker Bob Henn. This is where he got his first exposure to the hard work in the fields that is the essential precursor to successful winemaking. Later he obtained a degree in oenology at the University of California in Fresno, where he graduated with honors, followed by several years of training at the University of Bordeaux. His experiences in France have convinced Jason that Long Island needs to look to the maritime province of Bordeaux for inspiration, rather than California, since he believes that climatically and topographically there are more similarities between Bordeaux and the Twin Forks than perhaps anywhere else.

Jason wants to produce tightly structured, full bodied, and age-worthy wines that can, after reposing in a cellar over a span of time, eventually ripen into deeply rewarding and long lasting wines. This poses a dilemma for him since he feels the marketplace wants wines that are more immediately accessible. This dilemma is faced by a number of Long Island wineries. A compromise is not always easily obtained except by offering a wide selection of wines, some of which provide immediate and pleasurable consumption while others are for the more patient drinker who is willing to let the wine evolve in bottle for several years before pulling a cork. The winery's schizophrenia is reflected to some extent by the attractive labels on the bottles. They range from the bucolic simplicity of waddling ducks in one case to the more sophisticated image, on another label, of a sleek society matron and her beau driving carefree in an elegant roadster of the twenties, presumably on their way to one of the elite enclaves of those days in the Hamptons.

The reserve merlot and cabernet sauvignon are concentrated and brooding wines. Although Duck Walk may seem like a frolicsome name, the top wines made here are serious stuff. Jason himself is now proprietor of a new high density vineyard site in Jamesport that will allow him to more amply fulfill his personal ambitions for crafting large scale wines. It will be known as Jason's vineyard.

In the attractively spacious, high-ceilinged and airy tasting room one can sample not only the ubiquitous merlot, cabernet sauvignon, and chardonnay that are the staples of Long Island wineries, but also an unusual fruity red from the uncommon pinot meunier, a grape that is most typically blended with other varietals in the making of champagne and is rarely seen standing alone, as well as a pinot gris, first introduced in 1999. Additionally, there are two dessert wines, a most agreeable late harvest gewürztraminer called Aphrodite, and a surprisingly good port made from Maine blueberries, in addition to more straightforward but crowd pleasing wines such as Windmill Blush and Gatsby Red that are blends of various grapes. Since Duck Walk is under the proprietorship of Damianos père, some of the winemaking philosophy in favor at Pindar had crept into those made at the South Fork facility. This is especially noticeable in the creamy but noticeably oaked Chardonnay Reserve that is favored by many consumers.

The expansion of the winery continues unabated with new vineyard acquisitions that will enhance the growth not only of the parent Pindar, but also its offspring Duck Walk, surging forward while maintaining a wary eye on the competition.

Duck Walk Vineyards

Address: 231 Montauk Highway, Watermill
Owner: Herodotus Damianos
Winemaker: Jason Damianos
General Manager: Alex Damianos
Vineyard Manager: Reed Jarvis
Phone: (631) 726-7555
Web-site: www.duckwalk.com

Dzugas Vineyards

At a time when well funded and large scaled wineries are beginning to join Pindar Vineyards as major players in the Long Island wine sweepstakes, it is pleasant to note that small family-run operations are not only still thriving but growing. Along with Ternhaven Cellars, Dzugas Vineyards is arguably the smallest operation on the twin forks, with an annual production of only 400 cases. The owners, Donna and Stephen Dzugas-Smith bought nearly 30 acres of land in Southold at auction in 1993. Seven acres that were planted to vine by grower David Mudd in 1980 have now grown to ten acres. These are surrounded by organic farmland that will gradually be converted, in part at least, to additional vines.

Donna and her husband had no previous background in viticulture and bought the property "to gain a new experience," as Donna puts it. Fortunately, an early mentor was Larry Perrine, the respected winemaker who is now a managing partner at Channing Daughters on the South Fork, and he was instrumental in guiding the budding wine entrepreneurs through their formative years. This is a family operation, however, with Donna, the mother of three small children (one of whom is depicted on the label), serving as vineyard manager. They grow merlot and chardonnay, and it was Larry who suggested that they produce a chardonnay fermented in stainless steel to produce a crisp and focused wine that would preserve the varietal character of the grapes cultivated from some of the oldest vines on Long Island. Current vintages of the chardonnay have been smooth textured and refined. Beginning with the 1995 vintage the wines have been crafted by the esteemed Kip Bedell at Bedell Cellars.

Donna Dzugas with Derek, Brittany, and Kyle

85

In a region that remembers the Indian tribes that were indigenous to Long Island by dedicating towns, water bodies, and roads in their name, it is entirely appropriate that the new tasting room of Dzugas on Route 48, first opened in 2000, is a log cabin hand-crafted by builders from the Oneida Indian tribe in upstate New York. Though the Dzugas enterprise may be modest in scope, it's zest and originality have brought them to the attention of many wine consumers.

Dzugas Vineyards

Address: 4200 Route 48, Southold
Owners: Donna and Steven Dzugas-Smith
Winemaker: Kip Bedell
Vineyard Manager: Donna Dzugas-Smith
Phone: (631) 765-3692

Images of the East End

Peconic Bay Vineyards

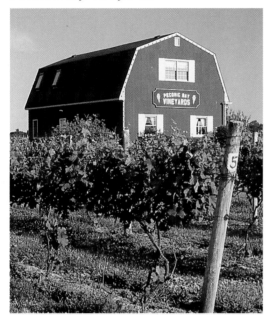

Farm between Pindar and Lenz

Pugliese Vineyards tasting room and winery

Ripe chardonnay grapes at Macari Vineyards

Duck Walk Vineyards

Images of the East End

Peconic Bay Vineyards

Farm between Pindar and Lenz

Pugliese Vineyards tasting room and winery

Digging for clams near East Marion

Grapes at Wolffer Estates–Sagpond Vineyards

On the way to the winery

THE WINES OF LONG ISLAND

Ripe chardonnay grapes at Macari Vineyards

Duck Walk Vineyards

Gristina Vineyards

Gristina Vineyards' main building, which houses the winery and tasting room, is located well away from Route 25 in Cutchogue on the top of a rise that initiates a long, undulating plateau. The establishment has engaged the attention of two generations of the Gristina family, but it is Jerry Gristina, the co-owner with his wife MaryGail, who is clearly in charge. Jerry bears something of a resemblance to a mature and wise family doctor. He is, in fact, a physician whose practice is in Westchester County and was recently recognized by *New York Magazine* as one of the best doctors in the Tri-State area.

There is a tremendous emphasis at Gristina on the vineyards. To Jerry Gristina, that is the heart of making fine wine, "It's effort in the field that counts. You've got to do it the right way in the vineyard." He initially chose his oldest son Peter to be vineyard manager. Though Peter toiled with patience and tenacity it ultimately became clear that his interests did not coincide with those of the rest of the winemaking team and he ultimately decided to move on to other interests. Today, Gristina has adopted a more aggressive approach to vineyard management than in the earlier years.

If it is Jerry Gristina who is responsible for the overall vision of Gristina Vineyards, it is Adam Suprenant who defines the vineyard's character through its wines. Adam, with a degree in viticulture from Cornell and another degree in oenology from the University of California at Davis, is the latest winemaker to follow Larry Perrine. An influential wine stylist, Larry guided Gristina's highly regarded early vintage starting in 1988. He is today a managing partner of Channing Daughters Winery on the South Fork. The reputation of Gristina underwent a brief lull during a period of family turmoil but that is very much part of the past and Gristina's wines are now better than ever.

The initial 30 acres of vines were recently expanded by an additional 34 acres purchased from an adjacent property. Jerry, who is an ardent lover of fine wine, describes himself as a wine collector who let his hobby run amok. He initially envisaged a country retreat, a place to have fun and entertain friends but it evolved into a substantial business instead. What is now the tasting room was intended to be his living room and Jerry's concept for the building was to combine the functional style of the Long Island barn with clean, glass-walled modern design. The large reception room with its high beamed ceiling was given a touch of warmth by the sofas and the rug in front of the large fireplace.

Jerry and MaryGail Gristina

The glass windows and doors on the north wall of the reception room lead out to a deck which overlooks neatly tended vines with lavender planted

between the rows and red and white rose bushes at their heads. This particular field of grapes teaches an interesting lesson about the effects of small variations in growing conditions on the growth of vines and the quality of grapes. To the casual eye the field looks flat. Some woods at the far end, a mile away, declare an end to the vineyard. There are, however, gentle undulations in the field, a rise and fall of at most thirty inches over distances of 100 feet or so. These barely perceptible hills and valleys create variations in grape quality. In summer, once you notice the variations in terrain, you can detect a corresponding variation in the growth and color of the vines.

Many vintners have clear conceptions of the wines they would like to produce. Those objectives are often based on wines they admire, such as the classic Bordeaux bottles in Gristina's collection that are rich but supple. Jerry expects the vineyard's reputation to be built on the red wines.

From their first vintage, Gristina's chardonnays have demonstrated complex citrus, melon and pear flavors and a fine balance: delicious wines. The emphasis, however, has been on the red varietals. The cabernet sauvignons at Gristina are intense, with Graves-like mineral and tobacco scents, and the merlots are lush and long. Both wines, especially those produced from the prime eight acre parcel called Andy's Field, are elegantly crafted. The designation "Andy" honors Peter's deceased grandfather who, as an octagenarian a decade ago, was a steadfast worker in the vineyards. Most recently, an impressive cabernet franc has been coming to the fore.

Jerry Gristina has his own version of the tug of war between the wines he most admires and what nature wants to produce on Long Island. For him the pinnacles of wine geography are the great red Burgundies, and he would love to produce wines from the noble Burgundian grape, pinot noir. This remains a troublesome and controversial grape on Long Island, however, in part because of its thin skin and greater susceptibility to any kind of fungal or physical damage. When Jerry started his vineyard, everyone told him pinot noir could not be grown successfully on Long Island. He took that as a challenge and set aside an acre to experiment with clonal varieties, the spacing of vines and vine management. He points out that the climatic conditions on Long Island are not that dissimilar from Burgundy, and no wetter than Oregon where some of the best Pinot Noirs in the United States are produced. Time will tell.

Jerry Gristina has an obvious enthusiasm for his vineyard and his own wines, but there is a deeper strand to his feeling. Once, when asked how he managed to combine the demands of his life as a doctor with those of running a winery, he pointed out, first of all, that it has been his income as a doctor that has supported the vineyard. Beyond that, he exclaims "This is the closest I'll ever get to being creative. There's very little that is creative in medicine, but we did this ourselves. It's exciting." "Each year we see a new beginning, a rebirth," he continues, and MaryGail, herself a health care specialist, concurs, "in our profession, we see disease and ill-health, but every spring the vineyard offers a new opportunity and a new challenge that differs from the year before."

Gristina Vineyards

Address: Route 25, Cutchogue
Owners: Jerry and MaryGail Gristina
Winemaker: Adam Suprenant
Vineyard Manager: Rob Hansult
General Manager: John Perry
Phone: (631) 734-7089
Web-site: www.gristinavineyards.com

Jamesport Vineyards

The barn that was reconstructed to become Jamesport Vineyards winery was built about 150 years ago. In what used to be the hayloft, one beam is carved with the names, Wayne and Abby, 1858. They probably were too preoccupied, blissfully one imagines, to conceive of the reincarnation of their potato barn as a winery. On another beam, two of the builders, Lefty Goldsmith and Wayne Tuttle, proudly left their names. A similar pride imbued Ronald Goerler and his son, Ronald Jr., as they labored to build a second life for Jamesport.

The history of Jamesport Vineyards is a reminder, as if anyone in the region really needs it, of the risks that accompany the winemaking business. Established in 1980 as Northfork Winery by an out-of-state holding company, it encompassed one of the largest and most varied vineyards on Long Island. However, the financial resources of the corporation were unable to support the cash requirements of wine production on the scale planned, and by 1986 it shattered into bankruptcy. Ron Goerler, an experienced businessman, was brought in at that time to pick up the pieces and guide the ailing corporation through Chapter Eleven proceedings. In return he obtained a majority share of the corporation's stock. In the end, the property had to be liquidated. Ron obtained full title to the barn and a few adjacent acres, but not to the vineyards themselves, which remained in other hands. This did not deter Goerler. He was already owner of some sixty acres in nearby Cutchogue, forty of which had been planted to grapes in 1982. Here was a vineyard without a winery and a winery without vines. The two came together as Jamesport Vineyards in 1989.

Ron is a canny businessman as well as a wine lover. Coming from an entrepreneurial background, including the ownership of a successful plumbing manufacturing company, he has adopted a tough fiscal stance to ensure that the winery remains a viable enterprise. As Ron puts it, "From a business side, I always like to make money.... You have to have that in mind, otherwise it's only a hobby."

The vineyards in Cutchogue, which include some of the highest slopes in the appellation (forty to fifty feet above sea level), are a patchwork quilt of several varietals managed by Ron, Jr. There are plots of riesling, semillon, pinot noir and cabernet franc, in addition to the usual merlot, cabernet sauvignon and chardonnay. But

90

the signature grape here, constituting about 30% of the vines, is sauvignon blanc. The cultivation of this varietal is especially interesting since it is conspicuously under-represented on Long Island; in fact several vineyards in the area have torn out their early plantings of this grape and replaced it with other varietals. However, the Goerlers believe that a fine sauvignon banc can be grown here, and they argue that its conspicuous lack of success until now has been due to poor clones and inappropriately chosen planting sites, and they have been determined to rectify this.

The winemaker at Jameport is Sean Capiaux, who has an oenology degree from the University of California at Fresno. Capiaux also owns a small winery in California's Sonoma Valley that is devoted to pinot noir.

Sean is somewhat skeptical of what he sees as "merlot mania" on Long Island and, contrary to the opinion often heard at other wineries that Long Island is climatically similar to the maritime area of Bordeaux, which justifies the large plantings of merlot and cabernet sauvignon, he thinks that "the degree days just do not add up." He counters with the belief that the Loire Valley in France is a more apt comparison to Long Island. Consistent with this perception are the recent high density plantings of sauvignon blanc at Jamesport, and the introduction of new clones of cabernet franc, both varietals that are widely planted in the Loire. Sean feels that these grapes can make wines of consistent quality on Long Island.

Capiaux's experience as assistant winemaker at the prestigious Peter Michael winery in California's Napa Valley, where acclaimed and much sought after chardonnays are made, has led him to apply some of the same winemaking techniques, including the use of natural yeasts, to the fruit from Ron Jr's carefully tended vineyard. His unfiltered Reserve Chardonnay, which combines a lush mouthfeel with elegant structure, suggests that he may be on the right track. Capiaux's fine sauvignon blanc is smooth and racy and it captures the distinct herbaceous aroma of the grape. He also makes a delicious late harvest riesling and an unusual port wine produced from the white pinot blanc grape.

Jamesport Vineyards

Address: Route 25, Jamesport
Owners: Ronald Goerler Sr., Ann Marie Goerler, Ronald Goerler, Jr.
Winemaker: Sean Capiaux
Vineyard Manager: Ronald Goerler, Jr.
Phone: (631) 722-5256
Web-site: jamesport-vineyards.com

Lenz Winery

Lenz is one of the oldest wineries on Long Island. The winery was founded, and the vineyards planted, in 1979 by Patricia and Peter Lenz after they sold their very successful restaurant in Westhampton, The Moveable Feast. From the beginning, their approach to wine was as a companion to food. Over the years, the Lenzs developed a series of well received wines, but in the late 1980s their energies and attention were drawn elsewhere, and while good wines continued to be made, the vineyards started to suffer from neglect. In 1988 the winery and its 30 acres was sold to Peter Carroll who already owned a 33 acre vineyard in Cutchogue. When Peter Carroll hired Eric Fry as winemaker early in 1989, and a new vineyard manager in 1990, Lenz winery was reborn, with a new outlook and an entirely new approach to its wines.

Despite Patricia and Peter Lenz's dynamic creativity, there was a dilettantism that pervaded the winery in their day. In contrast, while it may be a strange term to use to describe a small winery, we would now call Lenz thoroughly intellectual and professional. That tone starts with Peter Carroll, the new owner. Born in England and trained as an engineer, Peter is a management consultant during the week. It wasn't the romance of the wine business that attracted him, but the opportunity to run a profitable and interesting business. Whether talking about the economics of the wine business, soil chemistry and physics or the French concept of terroir, Peter is articulate and analytical, and so it is not surprising that when he was looking for someone to be the new winemaker, he wanted someone who had reasonably firm philosophies and opinions on wine. He also wanted someone who could "challenge the status quo and orthodoxy" that existed at Lenz. In Eric Fry he clearly found such a person, and someone with a compatible intellect.

Eric Fry is a fine example of the second generation of Long Island winemakers. In the mid-1970s courage was the primary requirement for someone coming to Long Island to make wines. Some would say you had to be crazy. By the mid 1980s, however, the region had developed a sufficient reputation to become a serious option for well trained, professional young winemakers, at least those with a spirit of adventure. Such a one is Eric Fry. After earning his undergraduate degree in microbiology from the University of Indiana, he took a job at the Robert Mondavi winery working on the problem of wine spoilage caused by a wild yeast called Brattanomyces. Eventually he found his way East, becoming winemaker at Vinifera Wine Cellars where he succeeded Konstantin Frank, who is known as the father of vinifera wine culture in the East.

When Eric first joined Lenz in 1989 he was thwarted from moving ahead with his own style of winemaking by what he has described as an uncooperative vineyard manager. The implications of that reserved characterization are that there were some knock-down, drag-out battles, and before long the vine-yard manager was replaced by Sam McCullough. The choice, apparently, could not be better. Sam has much the same philosophy of grape grow-ing and winemaking as Eric, who calls Sam a thinking vineyard manag-er. Sam owns 10 acres of vines on his own and the grapes he grows are made available to Lenz.

Lenz Winery

One of the most telling char-acteristics of the new Lenz is the strength and seeming stability of the classical winery triangle: owner/mar-keter, winemaker and vineyard man-ager. The fourth senior member of the Lenz team is Tom Morgan, the only remaining stalwart from the early days. Tom sits with Peter Carroll on the sharp point of the triangle, and is responsible for marketing and day-to-day management of the business.

Eric has made dramatic changes in virtually the entire Lenz line. In com-mon with a growing number of winemakers here and abroad, he has moved away from the big, oaky and exotic style of chardonnays once so common in California and Australia. He aims instead, in the Gold Label chardonnay at least, for a more Burgundian style of wine, one that emphasizes toasty and earthy fla-vors, rather than tropical fruit flavors; more "funky," as he once put it. Lately he has been striving for even clearer flavor definition and greater balance. The White Label chardonnay is an elegant expression of this varietal, a lovely blend of apple and pear flavors. The Gold Label version is a bit richer but still manages to avoid any suggestion of being blouzy or overblown. Eric also admires Alsatian wines and a tasting of his gewürztraminer and pinot gris revealed wines very

93

Alsatian in style, with a distinctive earthy mineral tang.

Merlot is the signature wine at Lenz and Eric feels it can be matched against merlots from anywhere. In some vintages they are big and lush, with great length and, as if to vindicate Eric's claim, a panel of tasters was not able to distinguish Lenz's 1993 and 1995 merlots in a blind tasting against the prestigious (and very expensive) French merlot from the same vintages that is bottled as Château Pétrus. The panel rated both wines essentially the same, with no clear favorites, an impressive accolade.

When it comes to cabernet sauvignon, Eric feels that although the fruit can ripen well enough, tannins tend to be marginally ripe, even in a good year like 1997. Therefore, after crushing the grapes, he initially does a cold maceration to extract color and soluable mild tannins, while sacrificing some structure which he then restores by blending in a substantial amount of merlot, resulting in a bigger and richer wine. "There are only two places in the world where merlot dominates cabernet, Peconic and Pomerol, just the opposite of the rest of the world," exclaims Eric.

Lenz Winery constitutes one of the region's most imaginative adaptations of local farm architecture to the needs of a winery. A group of farm buildings are clustered around a courtyard which is entered through a narrowing tunnel in an ancillary building. There is the feeling of entering a separate, magic place, a feeling enhanced by stylistic elements such as trellises and cupolas. Over the door to the tasting room, the visitor passes under a huge vine. Although not from the noble Vitis vinifera family, this riparia vine has its own reason for fame. Vitis riparia was one of the most successful native American species used as a root stock in the nineteenth century to save the French wine industry from destruction from the phylloxera epidemic. Without that intervention French wines might have evolved quite differently, and the Long Island wine industry, influenced as it is by France, may never have developed. So as you pass under this vine, give a thankful nod in its direction.

Lenz Winery

Address: Route 25, Peconic
Owner: Peter Carroll
Winemaker: Eric Fry
Vineyard Manager: Sam McCullough
Marketing Director: Tom Morgan
Phone: (631) 734-6010
Web-site: www.lenzwine.com

94

Lieb Cellars

PINOT BLANC

NORTH FORK
O IONG SIAND

1998

B

When Mark and Kathy Lieb purchased their property in 1992 on Oregon Road and Bridge Lane in Cutchogue, they acquired one of the oldest vineyards on Long Island, first planted by David Mudd in 1982. A sizable portion of that vineyard, whose original 36 acres has grown to 50 acres with recent acquisitions, is planted to pinot blanc. This grape makes what is undoubtedly the signature wine at this property; it is smooth, crisp, and nicely balanced, with subtle melon and pear nuances.

Mark Lieb is a money manager who lives with his family in an attractive contemporary home amid the vines off Oregon Road even though his firm is located in Connecticut. Mark initially sold his grapes to Palmer Vineyards and to other wineries but, being an avid wine buff, couldn't resist producing his own wine starting with the 1997 vintage. He deliberately maintains a relatively small production of three to four thousand cases annually, bottling only those wines that he feels deserve to be designated as "Reserve." The range is limited to chardonnay, merlot and pinot blanc, with a small quantity of sparkling wine. The latter is crafted from the pinot blanc grape by Eric Fry at Lenz Vineyards but otherwise the wines are made by Russell Hearn at the newly formed Premium Wine Group, a custom winemaking facility in Mattituck which counts Lieb as a major investor.

Mark feels that the vines, located just south of a bluff overlooking Long Island Sound at a relatively high elevation, benefit from the gentle breezes and moderating temperatures provided by the proximity of the sea and that this is reflected in the wines. His elegant label and unusually shaped bottles were chosen to conform with Mark's vision of an upscale winery. "I want the packaging to make a statement", he says.

The wines are being sold out of the tasting room at the Premium Wine Group on Route 48.

Lieb Cellars
Address: Oregon Road, Cutchogue
Owners: Mark and Kathy Lieb
Winemaker: Premium Wine Group
Vineyard Manager: Ray Hines
Phone: (631) 734-1100
Web-site: www.liebcellars.com

Macari Vineyards

The breezy and contemporary looking winery that lies just off Sound Avenue in Mattituck rose from the ashes of the former Mattituck Hills winery, whose bankruptcy in 1994 provided a unique opportunity for New York City real estate developer Joseph Macari, Sr. Macari's family had been holding 360 acres of land adjacent to the Mattituck property for nearly 40 years. The sudden availability of this once well regarded winery was timely since Macari had been contemplating starting a wine venture himself at that time. As it happens most of the Mattituck vineyards were sold off to the Duck Walk winery on the South Fork, and so Macari and his son, Joseph Jr, after acquiring the winery from the bank and winemaking equipment at auction, embarked on a program of new plantings that today includes about 220 acres of cultivated land. The previous winery building was redesigned and enlarged into the sleek tasting room that one sees today. It opened in 1998.

The striking new vineyards extend to the spectacular bluffs that overlook Long Island Sound. A largely, if not totally, organic style of farming is used here in which herbicides and artificial fertilizers are effectively banned, especially in the most recent plantings. What you see instead are great mounds of compost and manure on nearby fallow land that is used to supply nutrients to the vines; rows of marigolds surrounding vineyard plots to attract insects that, in turn, help control harmful pests; finely crushed oyster shells for calcium enrichment; and the use of a tractor-drawn flamethrower to scorch and kill unwanted weeds at the base of the vines. This, together with low-yield high density plantings of vines trained as low bushes and vines of varietals such as malbec, syrah, and viognier, each surrounded by small stones and pebbles strewn on the soil to reflect the sun's heat onto the plant, all add up to an obsession that the Macaris have with a natural style of viticulture that preserves the ecological well-being of their land. It will be fascinating to watch the fruits of this endeavor over the next several years. The highly capable vineyard manager is Bernard Ramis who has extensive experience as a viticulturist in the Languedoc region of France.

The first significant vintage here was 1997. The most impressive wines so far are the Estate and Reserve chardonnays, the first of which is essentially fer-

*Macari
Vineyards*

mented in stainless steel while the second is barrel fermented. The emphasis of
Gilles Martin, who was winemaker until 1999, was on a moderate use of new
oak to achieve a rounded and subtly aromatic style of chardonnay. There is also
an engaging cabernet franc and impressive releases of white wines made from
pinot blanc and sauvignon blanc. Although the chardonnays are currently the
flagship wines at Macari, it may well be that that viognier, a grape that can produce an almost excessively aromatic wine in other parts of the world, will
emerge at Macari as a most intriguing dry white wine. Macari's Marketing
Director Ryan Quinn describes the wine as "white peaches and cream." A early
tasting of a new Bordeaux style blend called "Bergen Road" exhibits luscious
fruit. Future releases will include a wine made from new plantings of syrah.

Macari Vineyards

Address: 150 Bergen Avenue, Mattituck
Owner: Joseph Macari, Sr.
President: Joseph Macari, Jr.
Marketing Director: Ryan Quinn
Vineyard Manager: Bernard Ramis
Winemaker: in transition.
Phone: (631) 298-0100
Web-site: www.macariwines.com

97

Old Brookville Vineyards

OLD BROOKVILLE
Chardonnay
1998
LONG ISLAND - NEW YORK

The Old Brookville Vineyard is altogether atypical of Long Island. There are no converted potato barns and rustic tasting rooms here. A somber, unmarked gate swings open off Cedar Swamp Road in the exclusive residential area of Old Brookville in Nassau County to usher a visitor into the palatial estate. A long road winds past 127 immaculately kept acres of rolling meadow and woodland until it reaches the 60 room manor house, once owned by the widow of Alfred Vanderbilt. The Elizabethan style mansion, with its slate roofs and cobblestone courtyards, is now the corporate headquarters of the vast Banfi wine empire. Just beyond the house are the vineyards: forty-two acres of high density plantings of chardonnay. One is struck by the similarity to the great châteaux of Bordeaux, the Loire or Champagne that hover over their celebrated vineyards.

No wine is made at the Old Brookville estate. Instead, the hand picked grapes are trucked upstate to the Château Frank winery in Hammondsport, to be vinified into chardonnay by Fred Frank, a Cornell graduate trained in practical viticulture at Geisenheim, Germany. Fred's father owns the winery in Hammondsport and the acclaimed Dr. Konstantin Frank, who first successfully introduced vinifera grapes to a skeptical wine industry in upper New York State, is Fred's grandfather. Dr. Frank was instrumental in persuading Alex Hargrave to come to Long Island. After Dr. Frank's death, Eric Fry, now winemaker at Lenz, took his position. It is intriguing to note how the Banfi vines are entwined with the story of Long Island wines.

Total production is small, averaging somewhat over 1,200 cases, and distribution is largely limited to the New York City area. In spite of an aggressive sales force, the Old Brookville Vineyards are in truth a minor corporate interest at Banfi, whose worldwide holdings dwarf the Long Island enterprise. In Montalcino, Italy, for example, an enormous wine estate releases a wide array of wines including the prestigious and much awarded Brunello di Montalcino. Apparently, the main reason for the Long Island vineyard is to keep forty-two acres of prime land in a rural state and out of the hands of developers; a shrewd public relations move that endears Banfi to the surrounding community. It is also an ornament, a charming conceit, to maintain the illusion of a titled estate. The mansion astride rolling fields and vines enhances the corporate image. It titillates the frequent guests and serves, additionally, to give the sales staff a first hand taste of viticulture.

Old Brookville Vineyards

The vineyards were the idea of the Banfi owners, John and Harry Mariani, who did the first plantings in 1982 after they purchased an adjacent property, then known as Young's Farms. A curious aspect of this vineyard is its proximity to New York City, the hub of the fine trade in the United States. No other vineyard of this size is planted so close to the city's center.

It also takes all the skill and dedication of Bob Whiting, the Old Brookville estate manager, to cultivate the grapes in an area that has a shorter growing season than the North Fork but the resulting "Old Brookville Chardonnay" displays fine varietal character.

Old Brookville Vineyards

Address: 1111 Cedar Swamp Road, Old Brookville
Owners: Mariani family/Banfi Vintners
General Manager: Bob Whiting
Phone: (800) 645-6511 x571
Website: www.banfivintners.com
Special note: The property does not have a tasting room and is not open to the public for tours

Osprey's Dominion

It is not hard to notice that nearly all the Long Island wineries are owned, and in most cases operated, by a single family. An exception to this is Osprey's Dominion on the North Fork. Bud Koehler and Bill Tyree are early childhood friends from Long Island who each seperately became highly successful contractors and sometime partners in construction ventures (Bill is now retired). They have also shared a lifetime of interests together including acrobatic and stunt flying (Bill owns an open cockpit biplane, the old Navy Stearman trainer, and Bud flies a Russian Sukhoi). As an aside, it is a curious fact that, at least when this was written, each has 23 grandchildren with the same number of boys and girls.

Osprey's Dominion

When it comes to wines Bill and Bud have delegated the responsibilities to winemaker Peter Silverberg who recently joined Osprey's Dominion from Golan Heights Winery in Israel after training at the University of California's oenology school at Davis, Vineyard Manager Tom Stevenson, and General Manager Vince Panicola. Although the first vineyards were purchased back in 1982, the winery did not officially open until 1996. In the interim, the grapes were sold with some of them used by Bud to make wine at home for the partners' friends to enjoy. Osprey's Dominion now produces some 18,000 cases a year from its 83 acres. The vineyards are not irrigated in the belief that the vines produce more flavorful grapes when they are stressed.

The classic Long Island varietals are cultivated here with chardonnay taking on a dominant role. In fact there are at

100

least five different chardonnay releases, including the well regarded Regina Maris, named after the old four-masted schooner that was long anchored in nearby Greenport harbor, and the impressive Reserve Chardonnay which is noted for its attractive citrus and melon aromas. The other wines from this property are also noteworthy, especially the lush and complex cabernet sauvignon.

Osprey's Dominion has positioned itself in just a few short years as one of the most significant of the larger wineries on Long Island and the consumer will do well to watch their progress as they hit their stride in the next few years.

Osprey's Dominion

Address: Route 25, Peconic
Owners: Bud Koehler and Bill Tyree
General Manager: Vincent Panicola
Winemaker: Peter Silverberg
Vineyard Manager: Tom Stevenson
Phone: (631) 765-6188
Web-site: www.ospreysdominion.com

Palmer Vineyards

Some would say that successful winemaking is mostly growing excellent grapes, and then mastering the technology of turning those grapes to wine. What is often forgotten, however, is that no matter how good its product, a winery must know how to market its wines to be successful. Today's wine market is highly developed. Vineyard owners from all over the world hire marketers and advertisers to sell their wines on the world market, especially in the United States, where they can realize some of their highest prices. This is even more the case in the New York City area where there is the highest concentration of fine wine consumers in the country. Palmer Vineyards has been able to compete in this world because of the acumen of an experienced advertising executive, the winery owner, Robert Palmer.

In 1978, Bob sold his advertising agency and with the proceeds in his pocket he started to look for land on Long Island on which to grow grapes for sale to wineries. He then realized that in selling grapes, he could be just as dependent on a few large clients, and just as worried about the consequences of losing just one, as he had been in the advertising business. This concern led him into the wine business where he would have thousands of customers rather than ten.

David Mudd planted the Palmer vineyards in 1983. While Bob Palmer produced some wine in 1985 for the wedding of his daughter, the first official vintage was 1986 when their first chardonnay and merlot was produced for public consumption. Palmer now produces about 20,000 cases a year. Bob's marketing skills, and the consistent quality of Palmer's vinifera wines, have earned the winery a place on wine lists throughout the country and his merlot has been adopted by American Airlines for their first class service. The region as a whole has benefited from Bob's marketing success.

The style of a vineyard is as much the doing of the winemaker as the owner. But winemakers can change, and such a change can be confusing to wine lovers who look for consistency over time in a winery's product. In some cases, however, what is lost in consistency is more than made up for in the evolution of the wine. Palmer is a perfect case in point. It can be argued that a succession of winemakers at Palmer has resulted in a product that would not have been produced by either one individually.

Gary Patzwald, Palmer's winemaker from 1986 to 1990, established a distinctively clean, almost austere style aiming for fresh, tart, green apple flavors in the white wines and, unique in the region, never used malolactic fermentation to soften his wines. When Dan Kleck became Palmer's winemaker 1991, he strove for darker, more complex, more highly developed flavors, and wines that were mature by the time of their release.   By a curious coincidence both Gary and Dan are now working side-by-side again at one of California's largest wineries.

When Dan suddenly left Palmer in the fall of 1998, Tom Drozd took over after having been assistant winemaker to both of his predecessors and, not unexpectedly, he strives for a compromise between the earlier winemaking styles, with a nod towards Dan. Tom is a native of the North Fork and remembers working as a youth on his grandfather's farm which, after being sold, was reborn again as Jamesport Winery. He eventually joined the Palmer team after spending a year in Italy and France during his college years where, as Tom tells it, he was inspired by the essential role that wine plays in everyday life.

Tom now works with not only the original 50 acres planted at Palmer but also the additional 40 acres that were acquired later from the highly regarded Ressler vineyards in Cutchogue. He feels that there is a distinct terroir to vineyards in and around Cutchogue, including those at Ressler, which produces fruit of greater weight and intensity than elsewhere on the North Fork, and the combination of grapes from both sites is an opportunity to make some distinctive wines. Although more than a quarter of the output is devoted to chardonnay, a number of other varietals get equal respect. Merlot, cabernet sauvignon, and cabernet franc are each crafted into generous and stylish wines. The Reserve versions of the same varietals, including the Select Reserve Red, a blend of all three, exhibit lush fruit and suppleness and, in the blend, a winning combination of cedar and mineral aromas. Palmer also releases a mellow and food-worthy pinot blanc, a grape that is seen too infrequently on the rosters of Long Island wineries, in addition to aromatic but dry versions of riesling, gewürztraminer, and sauvignon blanc that are each distinctive and fine.

Palmer Vineyards

Address: 108 Sound Avenue, Aquebogue
Owner: Robert Palmer
Winemaker: Tom Drozd
Vineyard Manager: Chris Kelly
Phone: (631) 722-4080
Web-site: palmervineyards.com

Paumanok Vineyards

Paumanok Vineyards is the epitome of the Long Island wine industry embodying the owners' enthusiasm for a life close to the earth, a lifestyle as old as civilization. Paumanok is the local Indian name for Long Island. In the choice of that name for their vineyard, and the care that they have taken to preserve the original barn buildings, the owners, Charles and Ursula Massoud, have shown their respect for the site's agricultural history.

The Massouds brought to Long Island not only their enthusiastic dreams of an independent rural existence, but also long family traditions in which grapes and wine were an integral element of civilized life. Ursula, warm and outgoing, recalls happy days of her childhood in southern Germany, working in her grandparents' vineyards. Charles wears serious looking glasses and has the demeanor of a careful scientist. When he and Ursula started Paumanok, he worked for IBM. He took early retirement from the company to devote his full energies to Paumanok where he now assumes primary responsibility for vineyard management and winemaking. Whenever discussions turn to vineyards and wines, relaxed smiles melt Charle's serious mien.

Charles Massoud grew up in Lebanon in its halcyon days and fondly recalls the sunny fragrance of his family's orchards. He learned to make wine in the most improbable location: Kuwait. The Massouds worked in Kuwait in the early 1970s. Wine was, of course, a necessity of life; a necessity which, in that strictly dry country, forced Charles to be his own winemaker. Grapes from Iraq were available in the local market, the souk. The Massouds crushed them literally by hand and, with sugar, yeast and informal guidance by other wine amateurs of the expatriate community, they eventually made a passable wine.

The Massouds came to the United States in 1978 hoping to make enough money to return to Lebanon to start a silkworm farm. However, in 1980 they read an article in the New York Times about the Hargraves and their vineyards. Charles traveled to Cutchogue to talk with Alex Hargrave and was so excited by what he saw and heard that he did not sleep at all that night. From that point on, the silkworms didn't have a chance; grapes and wine had permanently displaced them in the Massouds' dreams. Their restlessness was to recur for three years until, in 1983, they bought a farm in Aquebogue and, with help from Ray Blum of Peconic Bay Vineyards, planted their first grapevines. The hard work had begun.

Charles chose to plant his vines in a dramatically different pattern than was the norm on Long Island at that time. Instead of the usual grid of vines eight feet apart in rows nine feet apart, Charles planted his vines a mere four feet apart, thereby increasing the number of vines per acre, and the vines were trained to a single trunk rather than the usual two, following a common European tradition. With the single trunk system each grape cluster is fed by a larger root system.

Charles's early mentor in winemaking, "his teacher," he says, was Russell Hearn of Pellegrini Vineyards who remains as an occasional consult-

Charles and Ursula Massoud

ant. Over the years, through experience and by attending numerous seminars and conferences Charles has evolved into a skillful cellar master, as his most recent releases amply attest. Some of his red wines bear an uncanny resemblance to fine Bordeaux, with the pinnacle achieved by the "Tuthill Lane Limited Edition," a mostly cabernet sauvignon wine. Charles claims that this is a consequence of the fact that "our vines are older, our skills are improving, and the technology is better" and that "overall there is a better understanding of how to manage local conditions". These "local" conditions evidently include the fact that as one moves west to east along the North Fork, the average temperature decreases so that grapes in the western end tend to mature more fully. Paumanok, together with Palmer, is located at the west-most point on the Fork, in the town of Aquebogue, giving his grapes a ripening advantage of several weeks in some years.

The Massouds are indefatigable promoters of the Long Island wine industry, with Charles long having been the head of the Long Island Wine Council, an organization started in 1989 by Phil Nugent with the goal of increasing the visability of the region. Charles organized events that gave exposure to Long Island wines and he has been instrumental in enlisting more extensive press coverage than the region had been accustomed to receiving in the past.

From their 52 acres planted to vine, the Massouds release about 7000 cases of wine, including a refreshingly crisp wine from chenin blanc, a grape that is rare on Long Island. The winery has been committed to riesling since the beginning and it vinifies this grape in three different styles, from dry and semi-dry, to a late harvest sweet version that exudes orange blossoms. There is also a delectable late harvest sauvignon blanc with unmistakable quince-like aromas. The Massouds are especially proud of this wine since it was served at a recent dinner in the Clinton White House. The chardonnays are burgundian in style, with lots of finesse, while the red wines tend to have firm tannins and be rather intense, especially the Grand Vintage merlot and cabernet sauvignons, but these are always quite suave.

From their European and Middle Eastern backgrounds, the Massouds knew that building a winery would be a long and arduous task. Charles now acknowledges that "although in the beginning it was a gamble, it is now beginning to look like a business." Echoing a sentiment often expressed by wine growers, Ursula Massoud says, "You have to be in love with what you are doing, otherwise you couldn't stand it." Charles adds, "Grape growing teaches humility and patience. Our work will only pay back in the second generation, when our children have their children." This combination of passionate commitment and old world wine culture gives Paumanok a unique position among Long Island wineries.

Paumanok Vineyards

Address: Route 25, Aquebogue
Owners: Charles and Ursula Massoud
Winemaker: Charles Massoud
Phone: (631) 722-8800
Web-site: paumanok.com

Peconic Bay Vineyards

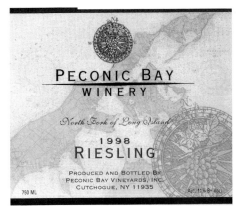

A visitor to the North Fork is conditioned to look for wineries along the north side of Main Road, Route 25, where most of them are located. Therefore, it comes as something of a jolt to see the tasting room and vines of Peconic Bay Vineyards on the south side of the road in the center of Cutchogue just opposite a shopping center. A converted farmhouse serves as a wine storage area and tasting room; nearby, renovated potato sheds house the winery itself. The thirty acres of surrounding vineyards were purchased by Ray Blum in 1979, although the first wine was not made by him until 1984. Blum sold the winery to Paul and Ursula Lowerre in 1998 but he continues to cultivate some thirty acres nearby. Ray remains a well known personality on the North Fork not only because his was one of the earliest wineries to be established here, but also because he planted, harvested, and managed vineyards for others during the years he owned Peconic Bay.

Paul Lowerre is an investment consultant in New York City who also owns about 150 acres on Oregon Road, at the northern end of Cutchogue. He put in place an experienced team to get the winery off to a fresh start. The vineyard manager, Matt Gillies, has worked for a number of the more important vineyards on Long Island since 1979, starting at Hargrave, and is currently responsible for some 18 acres planted on the Oregon Road property in addition to those surrounding the winery itself. Greg Gove, the winemaker, came to Peconic Bay from the recently reorganized Laurel Lake Vineyards and he too has extensive experience on Long Island having started as a cellar assistant with the Hargraves in 1984. Greg and Matt expect to increase the total acreage planted and to augment the current 8000 case production, with their first vintage as a team being 1999.

A sizable number of vines consist of riesling which is being crafted in an Alsatian style, with more fat and evolved aromas than is usual with this varietal on Long Island. Otherwise it is merlot that is being given prominence at Peconic Bay with Greg looking for velvety textures combined with as much fruit intensity as Long Island soil and climate will permit. This promises to be an auspicious new beginning for one of Long Island's landmark wineries.

Peconic Bay Vineyards

Address: Route 25, Cutchogue
Owners: Paul and Ursula Lowerre
General Manager: Matt Gillies
Winemaker: Greg Gove
Phone: (631) 734-7361

Pellegrini Vineyards

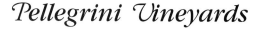

The large shingled building that gives the impression of a sumptuous beach front estate just off the main street in Cutchogue, the tasting room and winery of Pellegrini Vineyards, has come to be a familiar sight to visitors touring the North Fork. The interior appearance is something else again, a contemporary vision of a monastic cloister wrapped around a courtyard, as if to convey the message that wine is both hedonistic pleasure and contemplative joy. The building's balconies and connecting walkways are intended as a showcase for the wines and the frequent food and wine events that take place here.

Although the winery is new, the vineyards are not. Bob Pellegrini, a graphic arts designer with his own firm in New York City, had a long association with this area. Bob and his wife Joyce, a retired schoolteacher, first considered the possibility of a vineyard in 1981. Like other newcomers of that period, he sought the advice of the Hargraves, talked to David Mudd, then the impressario of vineyards, and looked for land. Eventually he joined forces with Jerry Gristina and together they bought the parcel that is now Gristina Vineyards. The partnership did not last, however, and Bob went off looking for new possibilities. After a long lapse, he finally closed on a thirty-six acre site in 1991 that, as luck would have it, is right next door to Gristina. When asked why he ever got into this business, Bob chuckled as he answered with a familiar refrain among winery owners: "You can make money in much better investments than a vineyard.... You have to love it and just want to do it."

Originally known as Island Vineyards, the parcel had vines on it that were planted by David Mudd in 1982 for the previous owners. Even though Pellegrini was late in arriving on the scene, the availability of mature vines on his property gave him a jump start. The porous soil gives excellent drainage, but as Bob points out, in arid growing seasons some of the vines can be stressed excessively. Fortunately, as often the case with vineyards established by Mudd, a drip irrigation system is in place that can be a boon in such unusual years.

From the original 29 acres planted to vines, an additional 35 acres are under cultivation from a property purchased later further east. The bulk of the production is in merlot, cabernet sauvignon, and cabernet franc, with lesser amounts in chardonnay. "From the very beginning we intended to be primarily a red wine producer," Bob explains, " and that is still the way it is." Lately, they have become particularly bullish on cabernet franc which is bottled as a single varietal, a growing trend among the Long Island wineries.

108

One of the advantages of cultivating a relatively small number of grape types, is that separate blocks of the same varietal can be grown in different vineyard sites, allowing nuances to emerge due to variations in soil and exposure. There are nearly ten different blocks of merlot at Pellegrini, for example, each of them vinified separately and not blended together until months after harvest. The blocks with the most favorable characteristics are the ones chosen to predominate in the final blend, like a painter who selects different hues from a palette of choices to create the most pleasing image.

Pellegrini's winemaker is Russell Hearn, formerly at Le Rêve, later renamed Duck Walk, on the South Fork. Russell received his vinicultural training in Australia beginning in 1980. Although Russell had been an interested and knowledgeable observer of the Long Island wine scene for a number of years it was only in the late 1980s, after having served as winemaker elsewhere in the United States, that he felt the Long Island region showed unambiguous promise. That is when he made the decision to move here.

Russell's approach to winemaking is as controlled and precise as his speech. His emphasis on control relates to his view of what he calls a typical Australian view of winemaking, namely that traditional practices should be employed if, and only if, they are shown to work reliably and have some technical justification, not because they have always been used. "I try to use tradition with as much technology as possible," he says. This doesn't mean that Russell is averse to risks but, simply, that he minimizes the chances of anything going wrong. "My job is not to make a flawed wine," he says in a modest and gross understatement of the quality of his products. His is an intellectual approach to winemaking that puts more weight on the analysis of past experience, than on either intuition or historic formulae.

The Pellegrini wines are stylish and well made. Both the regular bottling of chardonnay as well as the Vintner's Pride, an unfiltered chardonnay from closely planted Dijon clones, are excellent, but it is with the varietal reds (merlot, cabernet sauvignon, cabernet franc) and the Bordeaux-like blend called Encore, that Pellegrini excels. These are distinctive wines that boast ripe rich fruit, pliable tannins, and non-intrusive oak shadings. A late harvest blend of sauvignon blanc and gewürztraminer, called Finale, is a delicious dessert wine that should not be missed.

Pellegrini Vineyards

Address: Route 25, Cutchogue
Owners: Bob and Joyce Pellegrini
Winemaker: Russell Hearn
Vineyard Manager: Frantz Ventre
Phone: (631) 734-4111
Web-site: www.pellegrini.com

Pindar Vineyards

"Pindar in the ninth Olympian Ode, having had his poems scoffingly referred to by a senior and a rival as 'new wine,' says that he too had a reverence for old wine but preferred his wine to be fresh like flowers."
Alec Waugh, In Praise of Wine

Herodotus Damianos is a man of compact stature and vast energy whose vision and force of personality have had a profound effect on Long Island winemaking. A physician as well as the owner of Pindar Vineyards, Damianos has set Pindar on a path quite different from its peers on the North Fork. The most noticeable difference is one of scale. Rather than the twenty to fifty acres that are typical of other North Fork vineyards, Pindar now has some 400 acres under cultivation, and is still growing. Rather than fifty visitors on a summer day, Pindar attracts 500. They produce some 80,000 cases of wine a year rather than the typical 5,000-15,000. Of course, all is relative; in California, where several wineries produce half a million cases a year, Pindar Vineyards would be considered a middling boutique winery.

Some on the East End have been decidedly put off by the aggressive scale of Pindar compared with the normal, discreet Long Island winery. They object to all those tourists who on a Saturday afternoon pack three deep around the two-sided, forty-foot-long tasting bar, giving it the appearance of a popular Soho watering hole. There is something unseemly about the marketing push. Where is the Old World winemaking atmosphere? Pindar's detractors also take pleasure in looking down their noses at some of Pindar's products, particularly at the four popular seasonal wines: Winter White, Spring Splendor, Autumn Gold and Summer Blush.

"The Doctor" (as his colleagues at Pindar call Damianos) has another view. When asked what his favorite wines are, he doesn't hesitate in identifying Winter White along with his premium red wine, Mythology, as his greatest achievements. Mythology is a blended, Bordeaux-style wine, and is considered by some to be the finest red produced on Long Island. On the other hand, Winter White is a modest, inexpensive white; pleasant, but with little finesse or depth. To understand why Damianos identifies it as a great accomplishment is to understand the philosophy behind Pindar Vineyards.

From the beginning his long-term objective was to produce the "finest wine in this part of the world," and to "achieve national recognition," an objective unusual only in the confidence with which Damianos expresses it. This explains the creation of Mythology. But he had another ambition: to have a real impact on the Long Island wine industry and on the East End of Long Island itself. He speaks lovingly and protectively about that "beautiful and pristine part of the Island" and sees the wine industry as its savior. To have that impact Pindar has to be of a certain size; Damianos has to be a big player. Another mission for Damianos has been to educate Long Islanders about wine. The best way to accomplish that was not with some dry complex red wine, but rather with like-able whites. Ergo Winter White and its pairing with Mythology as an expression of Damianos's whole philosophy.

Damianos takes his educational mission seriously. Even now, he spends time behind his tasting bar, coaxing beer drinkers to appreciate wine. When they are ready, "the Doctor" will graduate some of his students and at the right time, move them on to the college level experiences of chardonnay and merlot. Some even enter the graduate school level of sparkling wines and Mythology. Damiano's educational objective also emerges in the Pindar tours, which over the years have been the most thoughtful and informative on Long Island.

Another factor in favor of Winter White was that when Damianos began planting in 1980 he recognized that his lack of experience and the immaturity of vines mitigated against trying to make serious wine contenders immediately. He did not want to run the risk of being criticized for having missed the mark. To establish credibility and cultivate a following it seemed like a good opening gambit to introduce easy-to-quaff wines, and this proved to be a winning strategy. Winter White has a loyal coterie of drinkers and it remains Long Island's most popular wine. The comparison with Mythology, which sits at the other end of the prestige spectrum, is that both are difficult wines to make. Mythology, as the flagship of Pindar's high end, cannot be allowed to falter. Although connoisseurs recognize that Mythology can vary from year to year depending on climatic conditions, it must always be in top form. Indeed, in some vintages Damianos does not produce it at all to protect its image. On the other hand, Winter White must unwaveringly maintain aromatic traits that the consumer can easily identify, year in, year out. Not an easy thing to do with a product of nature.

In 1987, aiming at a superior Bordeaux-style blended red wine, Damianos realized that he needed expert advice and engaged Dimitri Tchelistcheff as a consultant. Son of the famed enologist and wine consultant, André Tchelistcheff, Dimitri's experience was crucial in deciding what combination of the raw ungainly pressings in 1987 would eventually produce a refined red wine: the first Mythology. As the blended wine aged in barrels, there was some concern that it was not developing as expected. Then, according to Damianos, in late 1989, "Something miraculous happened. Suddenly, the elements came together into a wine of delicacy, balance and elegance."

The formula for Mythology has evolved over the years, and Damianos has been unstinting in planting Bordeaux grape varieties that can contribute to the blend. Originally, the predominant variety in the blend was cabernet sauvignon. More recently, cabernet franc has made up the largest fraction, with the next largest being merlot, cabernet sauvignon, petit verdot and malbec. In keeping with his goal of getting drinkers to gradually evolve to his top wines Damianos recently introduced a scaled down and more immediately accessible version of Mythology called Pythagoras.

With winemaker Mark Friszolowski, Damianos produces 17 different wines from nearly an equal number of grape types, including a sparkling "Cuvee Rare" sparkling wine and a decadently sweet ice wine from the riesling grape. Mark, a native of the North Fork, did his apprenticeship at Pindar and then moved on to Bidwell Vineyards in 1990 where he was winemaker for a number of years before returning to Pindar. To accommodate the profusion of varietals they have interspersed the original plantings with new rows to obtain vineyards with a higher density of vines. Among the grapes there are some that are largely or even totally unseen elsewhere on Long Island, such as pinot meunier, the traditional grape of the Champagne region in France, mourvèdre, a major component of wines from the southern Rhone Valley of France, and viognier. A recent entry in Pindar's grape portfolio is syrah.

Pindar Vineyards

Address: Route 25, Peconic
Owner: Herodotus Damianos
Winemaker: Mark Friszolowski
Vineyard Manager: Reed Jarvis
Phone: (631) 734-6200
Web-site: www.pindar.net

Pugliese Vineyards

ESTATE BOTTLED
1996

Pugliese Vineyards Champagne

Blanc de Blanc Brut

NORTH FORK OF LONG ISLAND

GROWN, PRODUCED AND BOTTLED BY
PUGLIESE VINEYARDS, INC.
CUTCHOGUE, LONG ISLAND, NEW YORK
ALC. 11.5% BY VOLUME CONTAINS SULFITES

A handsome burgundy colored sign on Route 25 in Cutchogue beckons one to the rustic tasting room of Pugliese Vineyards, which is partially hidden behind a country home on the road and by a large grape arbor which obscures the entrance. A small pond to the side of the tasting room and winery nestles next to another arbor that shelters a small picnic area for winery visitors.

Ralph and Patricia Pugliese, with their sons and daughter, have made this a family enterprise since arriving in 1980. Although it was supposed to be their vacation home, planting two acres of grapes in their first year seemed to be the natural thing to do. "I've been making wine since I was ten years old," says Ralph. He was raised in Brooklyn at a time when fathers and uncles made wine from grapes purchased in the market, and young family members joined in. Later, when he gave up his job as president of a construction union, the old Brooklyn traditions were taken east to a more bucolic setting. Here, Ralph maintains his direct approach. When a visiting French winemaker once chided Long Island vintners for calling their sparkling wine Champagne, Ralph responded by saying "In Brooklyn, if it bubbles, it's Champagne."

Ralph Pugliese with sons Lawrence and Peter

The roughly 40 acres of vines have been producing some 7000 cases of wine annually since 1986 and today it is Ralph's son Peter who is at the winemaking helm. Peter's brother Larry is the vineyard manager, both having learned their craft from Ralph. The family tradition that began in Italy and that continued with the newly arrived immigrants to America has been uncompromisingly maintained.

There have been some notable improvements in vineyard and cellar practices over the years at Pugliese but grapes are still harvested by hand and the wines are made with a

113

minimum of fuss. Some unusual varietals have been grown and vinified here, such as zinfandel and, most recently, the native New York State hybrid grape niagara as well as sangiovese, the primary grape in Chianti. Nevertheless, the traditional varietals continue to hold sway, especially chardonnay, which is fashioned into straightforward but attractively fruity wines. The signature wines at Pugliese, however, are the sparkling Blanc de Blanc (using chardonnay) and Blanc de Noir (from pinot noir). These are crafted in the champenoise manner in a cool cellar underneath the Pugliese home, and they receive considerable acclaim from the public and press alike. These modestly priced and inviting sparklers compare favorably with some of the more expensive champagnes around.

Among other wines sold at Pugliese are two uncommon items, a red sparkling wine made from merlot, and a sweet port from merlot and cabernet sauvignon. A home-spun touch at Pugliese is that the sparkling wines and ports can be purchased (at a slightly higher price) with designs hand painted on the bottle by Patricia. This is clearly a winery with a style of its own and it remains, as always, an unpretentious and refreshing presence on the North Fork.

Pugliese Vineyards
Address: Route 25, Cutchogue
Owners: Ralph and Patricia Pugliese
Winemaker: Peter Pugliese
Vineyard Manager: Larry Pugliese
Phone: (631) 734-4057

Raphael

Raphael is a nascent enterprise ensconced in a lavishly constructed building off Route 25 in Southold. Its architecture is an eclectic mix of Mediterranean influences superimposed on a sprawling building that is reminiscent of a medieval abbey, a place of contemplation. It is certainly the most opulent winery structure on the Twin Forks today. The owner is John Petrocelli, proprietor of a construction firm in Ronkonkoma, Long Island, and he named the winery in honor of his father Raphael Petrocelli who was an amateur winemaker in Brooklyn where John grew up.

Forty two of some seventy acres of adjacent land were planted primarily with merlot starting in 1996, in addition to smaller quantities of cabernet franc and very little cabernet sauvignon, petit verdot and malbec. From the beginning the idea was to make a single Pomerol-styled wine from merlot that would be labelled simply as Raphael, blending in smaller amounts of the other grapes to add nuance and complexity. The planting of grapes for white wines wasn't even proposed.

Petrocelli and his winemaker, Richard Olsen-Harbich, are convinced that merlot is the best red wine grape for the region, ripening sooner than the other varietals, and achieving levels of maturity that generally eludes the cabernet grapes in all but the most exceptional vintages. Staking the fortunes of a new property on a single product is a radical departure in an area where the wineries are accustomed to hedging their bets by making a wide selection of wines available to the public. Petrocelli seems to relish the risk, in keeping with his passion for stunt flying his Navy trainer, much like his friends Bud Koehler and Bill Tyree who own the nearby Osprey's Dominion vineyards.

Another striking change from the norm is in naming the wine after the estate rather than by the grape. The overwhelming majority of wines sold in the United States are labeled by varietal since this seems to be the way the consumers prefer to recognize what is in the bottle. In Europe, however, wines are more generally designated by the appellation of origin or by some other proprietary name and Raphael is observing that convention. It is perhaps not a coincidence that Petrocelli hired Paul Pontallier, the general manager of the esteemed Château Margaux in Bordeaux, to act as consultant. Pontallier evidently concurs with the decision to make merlot the primary grape here and is part of a team that makes no secret of its desire to craft a wine that outdistances the competition. Extraordinary care goes into vineyard management, nursing the vines through their cycle of growth, followed by a gentle handling of the fruit at harvest and during vinification.

These measures, in conjunction with a relentless program of pruning, leads Richard Olsen-Harbich to claim that the young vines on the property can achieve a level of quality usually associated with older plantings. Richard's mantra is to make wines that are "fat, supple, and elegant," a goal that he says can only be attained "by controlling the yield level and timing the harvest properly." Harvest timing means picking the grapes when they are physiologically mature, with just the right balance of acids and sugars.

Richard, low-key but focused and dedicated, is an experienced Long Island winemaker. He was trained in viticulture at Cornell and, after apprenticing under the famed German-born winemaker Hermann Wiemer in the Finger Lakes region of upper New York State, he became the winemaker at the now defunct Bridgehampton Winery. There he fashioned some of the most successful wines produced during the decade of the 1980's. After Lyle Greenfield's stylish winery closed its doors Richard joined Jamesport Vineyards before being recruited by Petrocelli.

One of the virtues of producing a single wine from essentially one grape is that separate vats of wine can be vinified from different parcels of the vineyard where disparate clones are planted. These separate batches are then either aged in new oak or in stainless steel tanks until the individual cuvees of free-run and press wine are finally blended into the finished product. This process of selection from the separate vats, the assemblage as it is called in Bordeaux, allows for a harmonious sum to be crafted from its parts. Those vats that don't make the final cut are blended together and sold under a second label. Wineries whose vineyards cultivate multiple varietals generally don't have the same luxury of choice available to Raphael.

The first release of Raphael from grapes grown on the property is from the 1999 vintage. It is still too soon to know whether the unstinting devotion of this relatively small winery to a super-premium wine will be fully rewarded, but it is difficult not to be impressed with Raphael's grand vision.

Raphael
Address: Route 25, Southold
Owner: John Petrocelli
Winemaker: Richard Olsen-Harbich
Vineyard Manager: Stephen Mudd
Phone: (631)765-1100

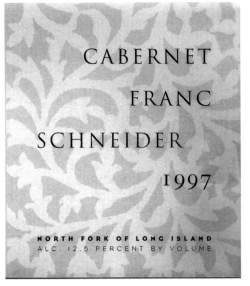

Schneider Vineyards

Now here is an interesting twist on the usual Long Island wine story. For the first few years of its operation, Schneider Vineyards produced several hundred to a little more than a thousand cases of wine annually without owning either vineyards or a winery, to say nothing about a tasting room. A young couple, Bruce and Christiane Schneider, driven by a passion for wine but constrained by a restricted budget, simply contracted to buy the grapes they needed, harvested them with family and friends, and then asked one of Long Island's winemakers to crush the grapes and make the wine to their (the Schneider's) specifications. The bottled wine was (and still is) sold to upscale restaurants and retailers largely from a website. A "virtual' winery, you might say.

This has not been as much of a handicap to the Schneiders as it may seem. By not owning property they were able to avoid an initial financial commitment and could postpone hard and sometimes irrevocable decisions such as what grapes to plant and where, while still learning the nuances of winemaking from other more experienced practitioners. In effect they avoided "getting locked in," as Bruce puts it, to accidental choices that in hindsight might appear to be less than optimal and difficult to disengage from. The downside of this, as Bruce admits, is that they have been dependent on the cooperation and goodwill of the other property owners and winemakers and, of course, their input into how the wines are actually crafted has been limited. Moreover they have missed the satisfaction of testing their own skills in the making of the wine. In spite of their unusual mode of operation the Schneider's have been gathering accolades from the press and are represented in some of New York's most prestigious restaurants.

Bruce comes from a family in the importing and distribution end of wine and so it was natural for him to have apprenticed in the cellars and vineyards of winemakers in Burgundy. It was then that he began to nurture the idea of owning a vineyard himself. Bruce and Christiane's awareness of Long Island's potential as a place to make this vision happen apparently came with a tasting of the remarkably good 1988 vintage, a benchmark year in which the public's recognition that something special was happening on the Twin Forks was first awakened.

The first Schneider vintage of 1994 consisted of a few hundred cases of cabernet franc and merlot. The 1995 cabernet franc produced from grapes at Gristina Vineyards and made by Kip Bedell brought Bruce and Christiane favorable press recognition. Bedell also made the merlot and cabernet franc from the 1997 vintage with grapes from Macari Vineyards while the chardonnay was made by Tom Drozd of Palmer Vineyards. The red wines are concentrated but supple and the chardonnay is stylish and complex.

Until quite recently Bruce had continued his studies at Columbia University's Business School and became the recipient in 1999 of a substantial entrepreneurship award from the Eugene Lang Fund that allowed him to purchase a twenty two acre potato farm in Riverhead. The Schneiders finally became land proprietors and were able to acquire their own winemaking equipment. The first plantings were made in the Spring of 2000

Bruce and Christiane Schneider

and although in the short term the wine will continue to be made by a consultant, a bona-fide winery and tasting room are expected to follow shortly. After the transitional period is over the winery will produce about 4000 cases annually.

Schneider Vineyards

Owners: Christiane and Bruce Schneider
Winemaker: Kip Bedell
Phone: (631) 734-2699
Web-site: www.schneidervineyards.com
Note: until the new winery opens to the public its wines can be purchased on-line at the web-site above or by calling the indicated number. They are also available at select wine merchants in the New York metropolitan area.

Images of the East End

*Corey
Creek
Vineyards*

*Grape leaf
and netting
to keep out
the birds*

Netted grapes at
Macari Vineyards

Tomatoes at Sep's
Farmstand in
East Marion

Entrance to Hargrave Vineyard

Old farm implement at Covey's farm

Long Island Sound from Macari Vineyards

The porch at Pindar Vineyards

Lenz Vineyards

Ternhaven Cellars

The smallest winery on Long Island. This is a distinction that Harold Watts, owner of Ternhaven Cellars, is not likely to lose any time soon. His annual production of some 700 cases of hand crafted wines pales in size to that of the competition and is no doubt marginally rewarding from a financial viewpoint. But Harold, a former Professor of Economics and Public Affairs at Columbia University, is primarily in it for the adventure. His five acres in Cutchogue, Wesley Hall Vineyards, are given over to the classic Bordeaux varietals of cabernet sauvignon, cabernet franc, and merlot. First planted in 1980, the grapes find their way into a handful of wines capped by Claret D'Alvah, a Bordeaux styled blend (claret is the older term for red wines from Bordeaux, and Alvah Lane in Cutchogue is where the vineyard is located). Until recently the wines were made by Russell Hearn of Pellegrini Vineyards but Harold is now fully in charge after purchasing some used equipment from a winery in Pennsylvania whose owners, long friends of his, were instrumental in nurturing his winemaking ambitions a couple of decades ago. Harold's totally hands-on operation takes place in a low tech winery located on the site of a former dilapidated gas station in Greenport (with the further distinction that his is the East-most winery on the North Fork). He uses a mix of old and new barrels and a modest assortment of equipment that includes stainless steel milk tanks that were converted into fermentation vats. Though his vines were planted two decades ago, it wasn't until 1994 that Ternhaven was born. In the interim he learned his craft by making wine in his Manhattan apartment from the Cutchogue grapes.

Although Ternhaven Cellars may seem to be an amateur's fancy, don't be fooled. Harold's wines belie their rustic surroundings and they compete seriously with those of his neighbors. These wines have garnered favorable reviews with their impressive aromatics and dense, plush, textures.

Ternhaven Cellars
Address: 331 Front Street, Greenport
Owner and Winemaker: Harold Watts
Phone: (631) 477-8737

The Old Field Vineyards

This family-owned establishment is still in the development stage, but its roots extend far back into Long Island's agricultural past. The first indication is the winery's name. It's not Old Field Vineyards, but The Old Field. That name was given to this terrain by the first European settlers around 1640, and indicates that it was probably farmed by the Corchaug Indians well before that date.

The basic motivation of Christian Baiz, the winery's co-owner with his wife, Rosamond, was quite different from other East End winery owners. A fifth-generation resident of Southold, his primary interest was to "find a way to make the land survive on its own." Potatoes and cauliflower weren't valuable enough and there was something "unaesthetic" about nurseries. When he read about Alex and Louisa Hargrave in 1973 he glimpsed a solution and, with the Hargraves' help, in 1974 he planted his first experimental vines on family land. In 1985 Chris acquired land at the west end of Southold where he planted 2 acres of pinot noir. For some years he sold his grapes until he realized that the profit was in wine not grapes. It was in 1995 that he produced his first pinot noir under The Old Field label.

Chris and Roz moved into the Baiz family house at the east end of Southold in 1996 and the next year planted merlot and cabernet franc in the actual "Old Field" just north of the house. Because of the fact that the vineyard is essentially surrounded by water on two sides the Baiz's grapes experience more even temperatures than are common a mere ten miles to their west. Since 1997, The Old Field wines have been made by Eric Fry at Lenz Winery. Their first merlot, a dark, concentrated wine, was from the 1999 vintage. The tasting room, along with a storage area, is temporarily ensconced in an old barn part of which dates from the mid-19th century.

If Chris Baiz has his way, The Old Field Vineyards will never be a big operation. He doesn't plan to exceed 10,000 cases a year of premium, mostly red wine. In this way he and Roz can keep control over the process and maintain quality. And make their land survive on its own.

The Old Field Vineyards

Address: Route 25, Southold
Owners: Christian and Rosamond Phelps Baiz
Winemaker: Eric Fry
Vineyard Managers: Rosamond and Christian Baiz
Phone: (631) 765-2465

Wolffer Estates-Sagpond Vineyards

Wölffer

1997
The Hamptons, Long Island
ESTATE SELECTION
MERLOT

ESTATE BOTTLED BY SAGPOND VINEYARDS
SAGAPONACK, NEW YORK, USA • ALC. 13% BY VOL. • 750 ML

On a quiet road just east of Bridgehamton, on the South Fork, a handsome villa appears amid a cluster of vineyards, home to Wolffer Estates known, until recently, as Sagpond Vineyards. With its mustard colored façade and light blue shutters, large earthenware jugs topped by cypresses on the front terrace, and antique stained glass windows, the estate looks like a cross between a Tuscan villa and a Bavarian country lodge. The cool and tastefully furnished interior resembles not so much a tasting room as the reception hall of an aristocratic European wine estate. Though the wood beams and large terra cotta floor tiles have the patina of a well worn but meticulously maintained private home, the whole edifice was in fact only recently constructed. A superb collection of seventeenth and eighteenth century wine jugs displayed in two cabinets of polished wood serve to enhance the impression of a well-worn residence. To the rear of the building is a vista of immaculately maintained vineyards, each row marked by a profuse rose bush, the whole more like a personal garden than a commercial enterprise. Below the reception hall the effect of order is maintained in the wood beamed ceiling of the cellar. All in all the atmosphere at Wolffer is one of serenity and gentility that sets it apart from any of the other wine properties on Long Island, excepting those at Old Brookville Vineyards where a similar atmosphere of country elegance prevails.

Not surprisingly, the presence behind this estate is indeed a country gentleman, the successful real estate entrepreneur Christian Wolffer, who bought the 14 acres of potato fields known as Sagpond Farms in 1978. By 1996 he had assembled 168 acres, which he devoted mostly to grazing land for his horses. Enchanted with the idea of a vineyard of his own after tasting a chardonnay planted by a Sagaponack neighbor, he devoted 50 choice acres to vineyards. His first release, a chardonnay, was in 1991.

Christian's European background is evident not only in the furnishings but also in his choice of winemaker, the young Roman Roth, who was born and trained in Germany. Roman was recruited by Wolffer after a stint as winemaker in Australia and California. A few years later Long Islander Richard Pisacano, who speaks of creating "balance and harmony" among the vines, joined the team as vineyard manager.

With the exception of a dry and very pleasantly aromatic rosé that is meant for immediate consumption, and a fine sparkling wine, the Wolffer Cuvée Brut, the winery produces only chardonnay and merlot, including estate selections of both types, each made in a full bodied but understated style that underscores the aromatic complexities of these varietals. Although the South Fork has long been thought to be climatically disadvantaged relative to the North Fork because of a slightly shorter growing season, it has now become evident through the accumulated experiences of the wineries currently located in the Hamptons that in fact the South Fork terroir may actually offer some distinct advantages. Roman explains that even in the hot dry summers that have blessed the region overall in recent years, the maturation of grapes remains slow and even ("there is longer hang time", he says) because the nights are cool, and there is a sizable drop in temperature in late summer. The ocean proximity also moderates the extremes in temperature between winter and summer. This permits the fruit to evolve in a more balanced manner resulting in elegant aromas, good acid balance, and milder tannins. This is apparent in the wines tasted at Wolffer, each of which maintains a certain toasty and creamy quality coupled with spicy aromatics and enough grip to suggest that they are best enjoyed with food. A vindication of this winemaking style is that an impressive array of New York's top-notch restaurants now include Wolffer's wine on their lists.

Adjacent to the vineyard, and also part of the Wolffer estate, is a large horse farm consisting of nearly 170 acres of grazing land and stables that shelter prized jumping horses among its tenants. At a neighboring dairy farm, one of the few remaining on the Island, a handful of cows provides milk that Roman Roth converts into a small amount of a mild but tasty cheese called Sagpond Farmstead. Another curiosity is Verjus, bottled from the juice of unripened and unfermented grapes that are pruned from vines during crop thinning, a month or so prior to harvest. Its combination of mildly tart and sweet flavors makes it an intriguing addition to salads or when deglazing sauteed dishes. The cheese and the Verjus are both available at the winery.

Wolffer Estates-Sagpond Vineyards

Address: 139 Sagg Road, Sagaponack
Owner: Christian Wolffer
Winemaker: Roman Roth
Vineyard Manager: Richard Pisacano
Phone: (631) 537-5106
Web-site: www.wolffer.com

THE CHANGING WINE SCENE

As this book goes to press there are a number of exciting new developments in the Long Island wine industry. Several new wineries were ready to be launched during the millennium year with others to follow shortly thereafter. At the same time, some of the venerable properties, past standard bearers of Long Island viticulture, were recently sold to new owners who have yet to establish their imprint. Existing winery names may change as, undoubtedly, will the varieties and overall style of the wines produced. In addition, a number of winemakers and vineyard managers are moving their talents to and from the new and established properties in a game of vinous chairs. Clearly the region is in ferment (pun intended) and it is necessary to wait and see how this shifting scene will settle down. We have attempted to indicate some of the upcoming changes in our winery profiles but the grapevine is a-buzz with rumors and uncertainties. The brief report that follows is a bird's eye view of some new wineries that are just now appearing.

Two startup operations can be mentioned, among the several rumored to be on the way. The wine importer and distributor Russell McCall has a property on Route 25, just opposite Pellegrini Vineyards, with over 20 acres already planted, primarily pinot noir. Entrepreneur Leslie Alexander, who is also owner of the Houston Rockets basketball team, is planting about 15 acres of vineyards in a recently acquired property exceeding 100 acres in Mattituck, along Route 48. He plans to produce a Bordeaux-styled blend based on cabernet sauvignon. It is not known at present when wines will be commercially available from these two properties.

Further along in its development is Martha Clara Vineyards, a sizable enterprise of 118 acres of high density vines along Route 48 in Mattituck. The land was originally acquired by Robert Entenmann, former owner of the eponymous bakery giant on Long Island, to be used as a farm for thoroughbred racing horses. The first release, a 1998 vigonier, was made at Wolffer Estates Sagpond Vineyards by Roman Roth, but future wines will be produced at the Premium Wine Group in Mattituck under the direction of winemaker Russell Hearn. The viognier is available at select restaurants on the North Fork. A tasting room is in the works where consumers will be able to taste a variety of wines from about 10 different grape types. Total production is expected to exceed 20,000 cases a year.

Laurel Lake Vineyards on Route 25 in Laurel is an established winery with vineyards dating back to 1980. The former owners sold the property to a group of Chilean investors in 1999 and the winery is now being managed by Cesar Baeza, a part owner and winemaker at Brotherhood Winery in the Hudson Valley of New York State. The roughly 5000 case annual production, most of it from grapes purchased from other growers, is expected to expand significantly in the first years of the new millennium. Chardonnay, the most frequently admired wine of Laurel Lake in the past, will continue to be produced along with wines from several other varietals.

Visiting the Long Island Wine Country

*P*lanning a trip to the Long Island wine country for the first time may appear daunting to the distant visitor unfamiliar with the eastern end of the Island: How do we get there? What should we see? Where do we stay? Fortunately, the wineries, except for Old Brookville Vineyards, are clustered in an area of manageable size; one can drive the entire length of the North Fork from Riverhead to Orient Point at a leisurely pace in half an hour.

From New York City and points west the usual approach is the Long Island Expressway (Route 495) taken to Riverhead, the town that straddles the base of the two prongs of eastern Long Island, the North and South Forks. If you are driving to the North Fork, follow the signs from Riverhead to Greenport and Orient Point along Route 25. This will take you past well over half the wineries, one after the other, in the villages of Aqueboque, Jamesport, Mattituck, Cutchogue, and Southold. If your first target is the South Fork, however, take Exit 70 on the Long Island Expressway south to Montauk Highway, and then go east on this Highway to the Hamptons.

From points north, in New England, there are two convenient ways of arriving: The car ferry from Bridgeport to Port Jefferson, and the car ferry from New London to Orient Point. From Orient Point there is an easy drive westward towards Riverhead, with most of the wineries along the way. Entry at Port Jefferson requires that one follow Route 25A eastward, past a less-than-bucolic strip of suburban development (although there is a welcome bypass to the town of Shoreham along the way) until the road splits at Wading River. Here one can proceed to the right toward Riverhead and Route 25, as above, or to the left along Sound Avenue. The second alternative is more scenic and leads past some of the other wineries not on Route 25. Sound Avenue and its continuation, Route 48, parallel Route 25, and there are frequent connecting roads between the two. The wineries are all clearly indicated by signs.

Visits to the wine country are most rewarding during the summer and early autumn months when the many farmstands offer a wealth of local fruits and vegetables, from berries to peaches to asparagus, squash, and cauliflower. Ideally one should plan a country weekend that includes both the North and South Forks. There are a few agreeable restaurants on the North Fork, and the wineries

Chardonnay grapes

can advise you depending on your itinerary. The posher and slightly less rural South Fork offers a wide array of dining experiences in the several towns that together comprise what is known as the Hamptons.

A lovely way to get to the South Fork is by car ferry at Greenport crossing Shelter Island, a ten minute trip, and then to follow signs to the South Ferry along Route 114. From here there is another quick ferry trip to Sag Harbor, where you can drive to all points of the South Fork within thirty minutes or so, from East Hampton in the east to Southhampton in the west. In between are the very inviting Wolffer Estates-Sagpond Vineyards, Channing Daughters Winery, and Duck Walk Vineyards.

Sag Harbor and the Hamptons offer attractive inns for overnight lodging (book well in advance) as well as antique shops and spectacular ocean beaches. The several charming inns on Shelter Island are especially recommended for an overnight stay because of their convenient location between the two forks.

# Bibliography

Adams, Leon D.. *The Wines of America.* McGraw Hill, New York, 1990

Asher, Gerald, *On Wine.* Random House, New York, 1982

Asher, Gerald, "A Vineyard by the Sea: The North Fork of Long Island," *Vineyard Tales: Reflections on Wine,* Chronicle Books, San Francisco, 1996

Asher, Gerald, "A Long Island Symposium," *Gourmet,* February, 1989

Beltrami, Barbara and Edward Beltrami, "A Wine Weekend on Long Island," *Food and Wine,* May, 1992

Blue, Anthony Dias, *American Wine: a Comprehensive Guide.* Harper & Row, New York, 1988

Darlington, David. *Angels' Visits: An Inquiry into the Mystery of Zinfandel.* Henry Holt and Co., New York, 1991

Ensrud, Barbara, *American Vineyards.* Stewart, Tabori & Chang, New York, 1988.

Gianotti, Peter M., *Guide to the Wines of Long Island,* A Newsday Book, Long Island, NY, 1998

Goldberg, Howard G., "As an Industry Matures, East End Vineyards Yield a Burst of Growth," *New York Times Long Island Section,* Sept. 19, 1999

Goldberg, Howard G., "Bordeaux-Style Reds Make Presence Known," *New York Times Long Island Section,* November 14, 1999

Gristina, Carol and Alice Wise, "Winery Industry," in *Blueprint for our Future,* Report to Governor Mario Cuomo by the East End Economic and Environmental Task Force of Long Island, NY, Newmarket Press, New York, 1994

Hargrave, Louisa, "A History of Wine Grapes on Long Island," *The Long Island Historical Journal,* Vol. 3 No. 1, p.3; Fall, 1990

Hiss, Tony, *The Experience of Place,* especially Ch. 7 "An Approach to the Next Generation," Vintage Books, New York, 1991

Johnson, Hugh, Vintage: *The Story of Wine.* Simon and Schuster, New York, 1989

Kramer, Matt, *Making Sense of Burgundy.* William Morrow and Company, New York. 1990

Laube, James, "Long Island Finds Its Style," *The Wine Spectator,* Nov. 30, 1988

Lawrence, R. de Treville, Ed. *Jefferson and Wine*. Vinifera Wine Growers Association, The Plains VA, 1976

Lee, Hilde Gabriel and Allan E. Lee *Virginia Wine Country*. Betterway Publications, White Hall, VA, 1987

Massee, William E. *Joyous Anarchy: The Search for Great American Wines*. G. P. Putnam's Sons, NY, 1978

Matthews, Thomas "Long Island's Summer Bash," *The Wine Spectator,* Sept. 30,1990

Matthews, Thomas "Long Island Celebrates Home Grown Bounty," *The Wine Spectator,* Sept. 30, 1991

Matthews, Thomas "Long Island's Work in Progress," *The Wine Spectator,* June 30, 1999

Morton, Lucie T., *Winegrowing in Eastern America*. Cornell University Press, Ithaca, NY, 1985

Murphy, Robert Cushman, *Fish-Shape Paumanok: Nature and Man on Long Island,* Waterline Books, Great Falls, VA, 1991

New York Senate Research Service, Task Force on Critical Problems for the Special Senate Majority Committee on the New York State Grape/Wine Industry. *Tending the Vineyards: Renewed Growth for New York's Grape/Wine Industry*. Albany, NY,1984

Peynaud, Emile *Knowing and Making Wine*. John Wiley, New York, 1984

Peynaud, Emile *Le Vin et les Jours*. Dunod, Paris, 1988

Pinney, Thomas. *A History of Wine in America*. University of California Press, Berkeley, CA, 1989

Rattray, Everett T., *The South Fork: The Land and Peoples of Eastern Long Island,* Random House, New York, 1979

Robards, Terry, "Zinfandel: the Mystery Solved," *Wine Enthusiast,* August, 1996

Robinson, Jancis *Vines, Grapes and Wine*. Alfred A. Knopf, New York , 1986

Robinson, Jancis Ed., *The Oxford Companion to Wine,* Oxford U. Press, NY, 1994

Wick, Steve, with photographs by Lynn Johnson, *Heaven and Earth: The Last Farmers of the North Fork,* St. Martin's Press, New York, 1996

Winkler, A. J. et al. *General Viticulture*. University of California Press, CA, 1974

Zweig, Michael "The Wine Industry and the Future of Agriculture on Long Island's North Fork," Research Paper No. 290, Department of Economics, State University of New York at Stony Brook, NY, 1986

Index

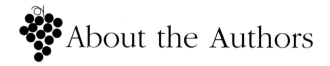# About the Authors

EDWARD BELTRAMI

Over the last two decades Edward Beltrami has written about wine for several leading publications, including *The Wine News, The Wine Spectator,* and *Wine & Spirits.* He lives in Setauket, Long Island, where he enjoys cooking with his wife Barbara. A frequent and long time visitor to the viticultural regions of Europe, he is a specialist on the wines of Italy. Beltrami is on the faculty of the State University of New York at Stony Brook and has published several books on applied mathematics, the most recent of which is *"What is Random ?"* (Springer-Verlag, New York)

PHILIP F. PALMEDO

Philip Palmedo developed his interest in wines when he lived in France for two years in the mid-60's. From the early days of the Long Island wine industry he appreciated its potential contribution to maintaining the special character of the East End of Long Island. Holding a B.A. degree from Williams College and a Ph.D. from MIT, Palmedo is Chairman of the consulting firm, The International Resources Group. He has written widely on subjects including energy policy, high-tech economic development, and the relationship between art and science. His latest book is *Voices in Bronze, the Creation of a Sculpture by Richard McDermott Miller.*

SARA MATTHEWS

Sara Matthews has been working as an international wine photographer since 1986. Originally from Atlanta, Georgia, Matthews spent her final year of architecture school with Georgia Tech's study abroad program at the Ecole des Beaux Arts in Paris, where she fell in love with food, wine, and her future husband, Thomas Matthews, currently executive editor of *The Wine Spectator.*

In 1986, the couple quit their jobs in New York and moved to a small village near Bordeaux, France for 18 months to work on their book, *A Village in the Vineyards,* published by Farrar, Strauss and Giroux in 1993.

In 1989 the couple returned to New York, where they have a house in Brooklyn. Matthews' work has been published in *The Wine Spectator, Food & Wine, Newsweek, New York Times, Saveur,* and *USA Today.* This is her third book about the wines of Long Island.

Long Island Wine Country

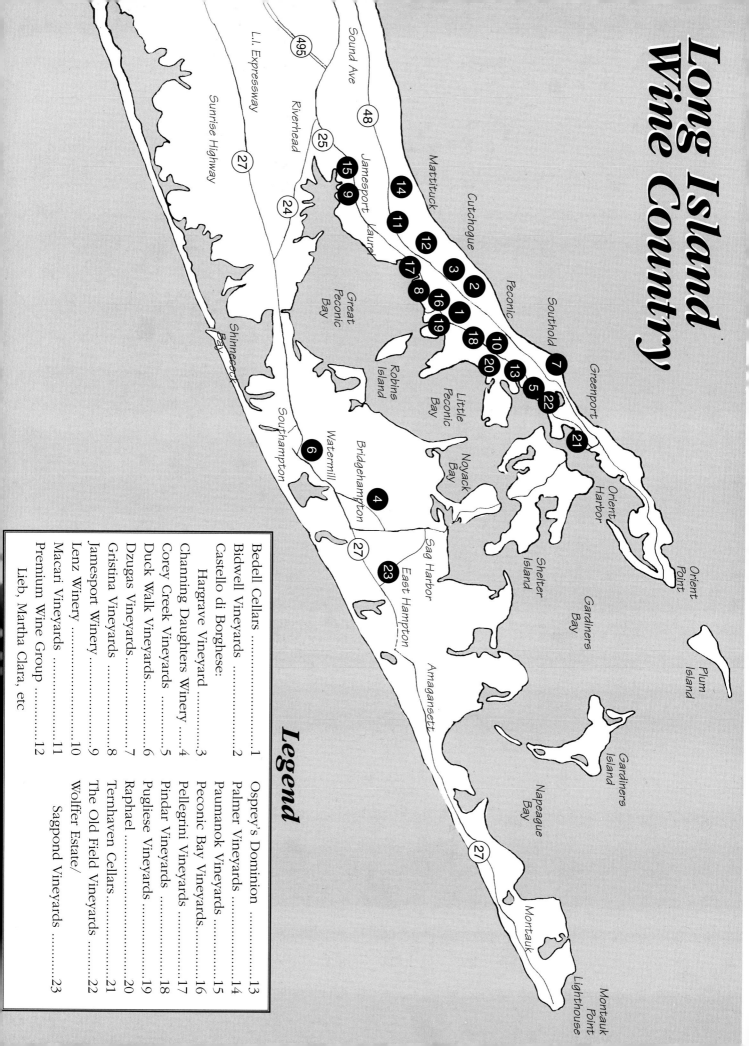